THE 52-WEEK DEVOTIONAL FOR NEW MOMS

5-MINUTE PRAYERS & DEVOTIONS TO RENEW YOUR STRENGTH, EMBRACE POSTPARTUM GROWTH, AND DEEPEN YOUR FAITH FOR A JOYFUL FIRST YEAR OF MOTHERHOOD

BIBLICAL TEACHINGS

_____

To

_____

From

Copyright © 2025 by Biblical Teachings - All rights reserved.

No part of this book may be reproduced in any form or by any electronic or mechanical means, including information storage and retrieval systems, without written permission from the author, except for the use of brief quotations in a book review.

Under no circumstances will any blame or legal responsibility be held against the publisher, or author, for any damages, reparation, or monetary loss due to the information contained within this book, either directly or indirectly.

Legal Notice:

This book is copyright protected. It is only for personal use. You cannot amend, distribute, sell, use, quote, or paraphrase any part, or the content within this book, without the author or publisher's permission.

Disclaimer Notice:

Please note that the information contained within this document is for educational and entertainment purposes only. All effort has been executed to present accurate, up-to-date, reliable, complete information. No warranties of any kind are declared or implied. Readers acknowledge that the author is not rendering legal, financial, medical, or professional advice. The content within this book has been derived from various sources. Please consult a licensed professional before attempting any techniques outlined in this book.

By reading this document, the reader agrees that under no circumstances is the author responsible for any losses, direct or indirect, that are incurred due to the use of the information in this document, including, but not limited to, errors, omissions, or inaccuracies.

CONTENTS

Welcome to Motherhood	ix
1. Feeling the Love for Your Baby	1
2. Learning the Basics of Baby Care	3
3. Finding Strength You Didn't Know You Had	5
4. Changing Your Life Priorities	8
5. Understanding Your Baby's Signals	10
6. Creating Special Routines with Your Baby	13
7. Balancing Closeness & Independence	16
8. Choosing How to Feed Your Baby	19
9. Solving Common Feeding Problems	21
10. Starting Solid Foods	23
11. Making a Sleep-Friendly Environment	30
12. Handling Sleep Regressions & Growth Spurts	32
13. Adjusting Your Sleep Expectations	34
14. Healing After Giving Birth	36
15. Starting to Exercise Again	38
16. Eating Well for Energy & Recovery	40
17. Finding Time for Self-Care	42
18. Knowing the Difference Between Baby Blues & Depression	44
19. Staying Present & Mindful	46
20. Managing Stress in Healthy Ways	48
21. Asking for Help When You Need It	50
22. Appreciating Your Body After Childbirth	52
23. Unexpected Body Changes Post-Birth	54
The Power of Encouragement	58
24. Sharing Parenting Duties	62
25. Staying Close Despite Being Tired	65
26. Supporting Each Other's Parenting Styles	68
27. Making Time for Each Other	70
28. Keeping Your Hobbies Alive	73
29. Setting Realistic Personal Goals	75
30. Staying in Touch with Friends Without Kids	77
31. Keeping Friendships Strong	79
32. Connecting with Other Parents	81

33. Setting Boundaries with Family	84
34. Giving Attention to All Your Kids	87
35. Changing Diapers Quickly	94
36. Babyproofing Your Home	96
37. Picking Baby Gear on a Budget	98
38. Dealing with Common Baby Illnesses	100
39. Budgeting for Baby Expenses	102
40. Saving Money on Baby Essentials	104
41. Planning for Future Expenses like Education	106
42. Balancing Financial Priorities with Family Needs	108
43. Choosing Childcare That Fits Your Values	110
44. Getting Ready to Be Away from Baby	112
45. Asking for What You Need at Work	114
46. Changing Career Goals After Becoming a Mom	116
47. Agreeing on Parenting Styles	122
48. Handling Grandparents' & Family Expectations	124
49. Celebrating Small Wins	126
50. Being Grateful for Motherhood	128
51. Finding Humor in Everyday Parenting	130
52. Accepting Imperfections and Growth	132
Pass On the Blessings	136
And So, The Journey Continues...	139

BIBLE STUDY
-Starter Kit-

Discover a **Simple**, **Powerful** Way to Study
The Bible

- *No More Guesswork* - Learn to Explore the Bible **with Confidence** and Clarity.

- Discover a Study Method That *Fits Seamlessly into Your Busy Life* - **Without the Overwhelm**.

- **Build a Bible Study Routine** *You'll Actually Look Forward To* - Not Just Another Task on Your To-Do List.

SCAN THE QR CODE FOR YOUR FREE COPY

WELCOME TO MOTHERHOOD

Welcome to *The 52-Week Devotional for New Moms*. The transition into motherhood is a profound journey that not only transforms your daily life but also reshapes your heart and spirit. Whether you are navigating the early days of bonding with your newborn or adjusting to the changing dynamics of your family, this devotional is crafted to accompany you through each step with spiritual encouragement and practical wisdom.

Within these pages, you will find a collection of devotions thoughtfully created to support you through the diverse experiences and emotions of new motherhood. Each devotion is grounded in scripture, addressing the real needs and challenges that new mothers face.

Motherhood brings an array of emotions, from overwhelming joy and deep love to moments of doubt and exhaustion. This devotional aims to offer you a sanctuary of peace, reflection, and growth during this extraordinary season. Each devotion invites you to deepen your relationship with God, reflect on your experiences, and embrace the new role you are stepping into.

How to Use This Book:

1. **Go at Your Own Pace:** Every mother's journey is unique. Set aside time daily or weekly to read a devotion, depending on your schedule and energy levels. Follow the order provided or choose the

devotion that resonates with you at the moment. Feel free to date each entry to keep a personal record of your journey. Remember, it's okay if you miss a day—God's grace is always present, and this book is here for you whenever you need it.
2. **Begin with Bible Verse:** Start each session by reading the title and the relevant Bible verse to set the tone for your reflection.
3. **Engage with the Devotional Story:** Immerse yourself in the devotional insight, allowing it to connect with your experiences and feelings as a new mom. These insights are meant to resonate deeply with your current journey.
4. **Reflect and Relate:** After the devotion, take time to reflect on the lessons and how they apply to your life. This section bridges the insight with your personal experiences. Use the "Mom's Moments" prompts provided for deeper reflection and consider journaling your thoughts. These moments encourage you to take action or reflect further, helping you connect more deeply with the topic. Engage with these prompts to explore your feelings and thoughts, and see how they align with your journey as a new mom.
5. **Prayer Time:** Conclude each session with the provided prayer, opening your heart to God, and seeking His guidance and strength as you navigate motherhood.
6. **Workbook Pages:** At the end of each section, you'll find a workbook page designed for you to reflect, journal, or take action based on what you've learned. Use these pages to apply the insights from the devotional and grow closer together as you deepen your connection with God.

Throughout these devotions, you will explore themes of love, strength, patience, and spiritual growth. From learning to care for your newborn and adapting to new sleep patterns to finding strength in unexpected places and balancing new life priorities, these devotions are designed to uplift and guide you.

This is a sacred time for you and your family. May these devotions become a source of comfort, inspiration, and spiritual growth as you embrace the beauty and challenges of new motherhood. Remember, God's love for you and your baby is steadfast, and His plans for your family are filled with hope and a future.

WELCOME TO MOTHERHOOD

Take the first step today. Open your heart, embrace this new journey, and let's walk this path together. This beautiful chapter of motherhood awaits you...

Welcome to the journey of motherhood.

P.S. *All scripture quotations are taken from the Holy Bible, New International Version (NIV), unless otherwise noted.*

The Early Days of
MOTHERHOOD

1

FEELING THE LOVE FOR YOUR BABY

___ / ___ / _____

> *"So, in the course of time, Hannah became pregnant and gave birth to a son. She named him Samuel, saying, 'Because I asked the Lord for him.'"*
>
> — 1 SAMUEL 1:20

The first time I held my baby, that tiny bundle of joy nestled in my arms and looked up at me with wide eyes, I felt an overwhelming love and a divine presence. I was flooded with emotions I had never experienced before, and tears of joy streamed down my face as I whispered a prayer of thanks..

In the Bible, we read about Hannah, who longed for a child and prayed earnestly for one. When God blessed her with Samuel, her love for him was profound and immediate. She dedicated him to the Lord, recognizing that he was a precious gift from God.

Feeling love for your baby is an incredible experience—a mix of tenderness, protectiveness, and responsibility. Spend quiet moments with your baby, holding them close, talking to them, and simply being present. These moments strengthen your connection and create a sense of security and trust.

BIBLICAL TEACHINGS

It's natural to have moments of doubt and exhaustion. During those times, lean on God's divine support. Just as God blessed Hannah with the strength and patience to care for Samuel, He offers you the same support. When the nights are long and the days are tiring, pray for God's guidance and strength. Allow His love to fill you, replenishing your spirit and reminding you of the incredible blessing you hold in your arms.

One practical way to feel and express love is through intentional prayer and reflection. Each night, as you lay your baby down to sleep, thank God for the gift of your child. Reflect on the joys of the day, no matter how small, and ask for His wisdom to guide you through the challenges. This practice can deepen your gratitude and help you focus on the beautiful bond you share with your baby.

Just as Hannah felt immense love for Samuel, our love for our children reflects God's love for us. Every cry, coo, and tiny movement is a reminder of this miraculous gift. Holding your baby for the first time, you might have felt awe and gratitude, knowing this little one is a blessing from God.

As new mothers, it's easy to get overwhelmed with the demands of caring for a newborn. However, it's important to pause and remember the sacredness of the bond we share with our children. Our love for them is a powerful force rooted in divine love, enduring sleepless nights, endless feedings, and countless diaper changes.

Mom's Moments

Today, take a moment to hold your baby close and whisper a prayer of gratitude. Reflect on the love you felt when you first held your baby and how God's presence was evident.

Short Prayer

Dear God, thank You for the gift of my baby. Help me to love and care for them with the same dedication Hannah had for Samuel. Amen.

2

LEARNING THE BASICS OF BABY CARE

___ / ___ / _____

"But Mary treasured up all these things and pondered them in her heart."

— LUKE 2:19

Remember those challenging moments of early motherhood: the first time your baby had a fever or those sleepless nights when you felt like you couldn't do anything right. Think about Mary for a second - a young mom suddenly tasked with raising Jesus. The pressure must have been intense. But the Bible tells us that Mary didn't feel overwhelmed. Instead, she treasured these moments and relied on her faith, trusting that God would guide her. She handled such a massive responsibility with grace, taking it one day at a time.

As you navigate baby care, there will be times when you feel unsure and anxious. The first diaper change, bath, and feeding can be daunting. But remember, just like Mary, you are not alone. God's got your back every step of the way, giving you the strength and knowledge you need.

To build your confidence in baby care, be patient with yourself and embrace the learning process. Every mother goes through trial and error. Celebrate small victories like successfully burping your baby or mastering the perfect swaddle. These accomplishments are significant milestones in your journey as a mother.

It's normal to feel overwhelmed at times. Don't hesitate to seek advice from experienced mothers, your pediatrician, or reliable parenting resources. Remember, even Mary had Joseph and likely relied on her community for support. Building your own support network can provide valuable tips and much-needed encouragement.

When you're feeling uncertain, take a moment for prayer. Ask for patience, wisdom, and peace. You might be surprised how this can renew your confidence and help you face challenges.

One practical tip many new moms find helpful is keeping a baby care journal. By tracking feeding times, diaper changes, and sleep patterns, you'll better understand your baby's needs. This can make daily care more manageable and help you establish a routine.

Remember, asking for help isn't a sign of weakness - it's a smart way to navigate this new journey. With time and practice, you'll grow more confident in your abilities as a mother.

Mom's Moments

Write a short letter to yourself celebrating your resilience and the small victories you achieve daily. Keep it somewhere special to read on tougher days.

Short Prayer

Dear God, thank You for guiding me through the challenges of motherhood. Help me to lean on Your grace and strength in every moment. Amen.

3

FINDING STRENGTH YOU DIDN'T KNOW YOU HAD

___ / ___ / _____

> *"But when she could hide him no longer, she got a papyrus basket for him and coated it with tar and pitch. Then she placed the child in it and put it among the reeds along the bank of the Nile."*
>
> — EXODUS 2:3

Think back to a time when you surprised yourself with your strength as a new mom. *Is there one particular moment that stands out?* I have one. My baby was only a few weeks old, and it was one of those nights when everything seemed to go wrong. My little one was inconsolable, crying for hours. Nothing I did seemed to soothe him, and exhaustion weighed heavily on my shoulders. I felt utterly helpless.

In that moment of despair, I remembered the story of Jochebed, Moses's mother. Despite the danger, she found the strength to protect her son. Faithfully and determined, she placed Moses in a basket and set him afloat on the Nile, trusting God to watch over him. Her courage and reliance on God inspired me.

I took a deep breath, whispered a prayer for strength, and kept going. I sang softly to my baby, rocking him gently, and eventually, he calmed down and fell asleep. In those quiet moments, I realized I had found a strength I didn't know I had. It wasn't just physical strength but a deep spiritual strength from trusting God to help me through the toughest times.

This experience profoundly deepened my reliance on the Lord. I learned that God's grace is sufficient even when I feel completely inadequate. Jochebed trusted God with her precious child, so I learned to entrust my struggles and fears to Him. Each challenge became an opportunity to lean more on God's unfailing strength and love.

To tap into your inner strength as a new mom, embrace those moments of weakness and use them as chances to grow. When you're feeling overwhelmed, take a moment to breathe and center yourself. Reach out to supportive friends and family, just like Jochebed had Miriam and Aaron. Lean on your community and remember that you don't have to do it all alone.

Practical steps can also help you discover and maximize your strength. Establish a routine that includes moments of rest and reflection. These pauses can recharge you physically and spiritually. Taking care of your well-being is crucial; when you are rested and centered, you are better equipped to care for your baby.

Another way to find strength is to remember your purpose. Just as Jochebed had a clear mission to protect Moses, understanding the importance of your role can give you the resilience to face challenges. Remind yourself that every diaper change, sleepless night, and soothing session is an act of love and dedication. You nurture a precious life, and that purpose can fuel your strength.

Mom's Moments

Today, reflect on a recent moment when you discovered a new strength within yourself. Thank God for His presence and support, and ask for continued strength in your journey.

Short Prayer

Dear God, thank You for revealing my inner strength in need. Help me to rely on Your grace and wisdom as I care for my child. Amen.

4

CHANGING YOUR LIFE PRIORITIES

___ / ___ / _____

"Her neighbors and relatives heard that the Lord had shown her great mercy, and they shared her joy."

— LUKE 1:58

How has becoming a mom changed how you view life and your walk with God? When Elizabeth, an older woman who had longed for a child, finally gave birth to John, her joy was indescribable. Her neighbors and relatives rejoiced with her, witnessing the great mercy the Lord had shown her. Elizabeth's priorities shifted dramatically as she embraced her new role as a mother.

Elizabeth's story is a beautiful example of how becoming a parent can transform our lives and deepen our relationship with God. Before John's birth, Elizabeth's life was marked by longing and perhaps even questioning God's timing. But with the arrival of her son, her focus shifted entirely. She was no longer just Elizabeth but John's mother, entrusted with raising a child who would play a pivotal role in God's plan.

Similarly, becoming a mother often brings about a shift in priorities. What once seemed important may fade into the background as the needs and well-being of our children take center stage. This new life in our arms reshapes our daily routines, goals, and even dreams. This shift can be both beautiful and challenging as we balance our responsibilities and personal aspirations.

Elizabeth didn't resist her new role; she embraced it with joy and gratitude, recognizing it as a blessing from God. We, too, can find joy in the new priorities motherhood brings by viewing them as extensions of our faith journey.

One way to do this is to integrate our walk with God into our parenting. Just as Elizabeth likely prayed over John and taught him about God's promises, we can make our faith a central part of our parenting. Simple practices like praying with your child, reading Bible stories together, and modeling Christ-like behavior can create a strong spiritual foundation for your family.

Additionally, set new priorities that align with your role as a mother and a follower of Christ. This might mean adjusting your schedule to include more family time, setting aside moments for personal prayer and reflection, or finding ways to serve others with your child. By making deliberate choices, you can ensure that your new priorities reflect your values and faith.

Mom's Moments

Write down three new priorities or values motherhood has brought into your life. Place this list somewhere you'll see it often. Create a small vision board with pictures and quotes that remind you of these priorities. Display it in a place you see daily.

Short Prayer

Dear God, thank You for the gift of motherhood and how it has changed my life. Help me to embrace these changes and prioritize my walk with You. Amen.

5

UNDERSTANDING YOUR BABY'S SIGNALS

___ / ___ / _____

> *"Sarah said, 'God has brought me laughter, and everyone who hears about this will laugh with me.' And she added, 'Who would have said to Abraham that Sarah would nurse children? Yet I have borne him a son in his old age.'"*
>
> — GENESIS 21:6-7

What signals does your baby give when hungry or tired? How did you learn to recognize these with the Lord's guidance? As a new mother, deciphering your baby's cries and cues can feel like learning a new language. Each cry, coo, and gesture holds a different meaning, and understanding these signals is essential to caring for your little one.

Sarah gave birth to Isaac when she was old. Her joy was immeasurable, but like any mother, she had to learn to understand her baby's needs. With God's guidance, she embraced the challenge, finding joy and laughter. As Sarah relied on God's wisdom, you can seek His guidance in understanding your baby's signals.

Recognizing when your baby is hungry or tired takes time and patience, but you'll get there with some practice and prayer. Start by paying close attention to your baby's sounds and body language. For example, a hungry baby might make sucking motions, root around, or cry in a certain way. On the other hand, a tired baby might rub their eyes, yawn, or get fussy. By noticing these cues, you'll start to tell the difference.

Having a routine can really help both you and your baby. Try to keep feeding and nap times at the same hours each day. This helps your baby feel safe and makes it easier for you to know what they need.

When you're not sure what your baby needs, a quick prayer can be really comforting. Ask God to help you understand your baby's needs. Remember, God gave you this precious little one and will give you the strength and insight you need.

Every baby is different, so what works for one might not work for another. Be patient with yourself as you learn your baby's unique signals. Over time, you'll get better at understanding what they need.

Don't be afraid to ask for help. Experienced moms, family members, and your pediatrician can offer great advice. God often works through others to give you the support and knowledge you need.

Documenting your baby's feeding times, sleep patterns, and behaviors can reveal patterns that help you anticipate their needs. This practice can highlight small victories and improvements, reinforcing your confidence and capability as a mother.

Additionally, create a peaceful environment that fosters clear communication between you and your baby. Minimize distractions during feeding and naptime, allowing you to focus on your baby's cues. This mindful approach can deepen your bond and enhance your ability to understand their needs.

Mom's Moments

Spend today carefully observing your baby's cues. Note how they signal their needs and how you've learned to understand them. Write down the different cues your baby uses to communicate. Reflect on how this understanding strengthens your bond and helps you respond better to their needs.

BIBLICAL TEACHINGS

Short Prayer

Thank God for helping me understand my baby's needs. Grant me the wisdom and patience to continue learning and growing on this journey. Amen.

6

CREATING SPECIAL ROUTINES WITH YOUR BABY

___ / ___ / _____

"Start children off on the way they should go, and even when they are old they will not turn from it."

— PROVERBS 22:6

Research indicates that babies thrive on routines that help them feel secure and develop healthy sleep patterns. Establishing consistent rituals can also strengthen the parent-child bond. Consider the routines or rituals you've developed to bond with your baby and how these moments reflect your faith. Think about the story of Daniel, who remained faithful to his spiritual practices even in a foreign land. His unwavering commitment to daily prayer routines highlights the importance of consistent spiritual practices, even in adversity.

Daniel's dedication to praying three times a day wasn't a one-time event but a lifelong commitment. His routines reflected his deep faith and gratitude, influencing those around him and shaping his destiny. Daniel's story reminds us that our daily routines and rituals with our children can have profound spiritual significance.

Creating special routines with your baby is a wonderful way to bond and make them feel secure and loved. These moments also provide opportunities to reflect and share your faith with your child. Here are some practical steps to help you develop meaningful routines.

Start with bedtime prayers and stories. Establish a nightly routine where you share a prayer and a Bible story to help your baby wind down and learn about your faith. This ritual can foster a sense of peace and connection.

In the morning, begin your day with a simple devotion. Sing a hymn, recite a verse, or say a prayer together. These moments can set a positive tone for the rest of the day.

During meals, say a blessing before eating. This consistent practice teaches gratitude and reverence, even if your baby is too young to understand fully.

Take your baby for walks and use that time to talk to God. Describe the beauty around you, thank Him for the day, and express your hopes and prayers. This routine can be calming and spiritually enriching.

Lastly, celebrate milestones and holidays with special rituals. You might light a candle for each month of your baby's life or create a thankfulness jar. These traditions can reflect your faith and joy, creating lasting memories for both you and your baby.

Just as Daniel consistently prayed to God, maintaining these routines regularly helps embed them into your child's life. It's also important to be flexible and adapt as your baby grows, finding new ways to incorporate faith into daily interactions.

Lean on God's grace as you develop and maintain these routines. There will be days when it feels challenging to stick to your plans, but remember that every effort you make to include God in your daily life with your baby is valuable. Pray for patience and creativity, and trust that God will guide you in nurturing your child's faith.

Mom's Moments

Take a moment to think about the routines you've established with your baby. How do these moments help you bond and share your faith? Write down the routines you currently have and those you wish to establish. Consider how you can incorporate these new routines into your daily life to make them meaningful and consistent.

Short Prayer

Dear God, thank You for the opportunity to create special routines with my baby. Help me to make these moments meaningful and faith-filled. Amen.

7

BALANCING CLOSENESS & INDEPENDENCE

___ / ___ / _____

"Jesus grew in wisdom and stature and in favor with God and man."

— LUKE 2:52

How do you show love to your baby while encouraging them to explore the world around them? Consider the story of Abraham and Isaac. When God asked Abraham to sacrifice his beloved son, Abraham had to trust God completely. While this story is often remembered for its test of faith, it also highlights Abraham's ability to let go and trust in God's plan for Isaac's future. Abraham's willingness to obey God, even in such a difficult situation, illustrates the balance of nurturing closeness and fostering independence through faith.

As a new mother, you might feel the instinct to keep your baby close at all times, protecting them from harm. This closeness fosters a strong bond and a sense of security. However, it's also important to encourage your child's natural curiosity and exploration, helping them discover the world around them as a creation of God.

Balancing closeness and independence is crucial for your baby's development. One way to support this balance is by creating a safe and nurturing environment where your baby can explore freely. By baby-proofing your home, you allow them to crawl, walk, and discover without constant restrictions. This kind of freedom helps them develop confidence and independence while knowing you are always nearby.

Encouraging your baby's natural curiosity is also essential. Introducing them to new sights, sounds, and textures can be very stimulating. Take them on nature walks, let them touch different materials, and describe the world around them. These experiences not only stimulate their development but also teach them to appreciate God's creation.

Being present and attentive is important, but it's equally crucial not to hover. Offering guidance and support while allowing your baby to try new things, even if it means making mistakes, shows your love without being overbearing.

Incorporating faith into exploration times can be a wonderful way to instill values. When you're outdoors, talk about the beauty of God's creation, pointing out trees, flowers, and animals. Reading Bible stories that highlight God's love for His creation and explaining how we are part of it can be very meaningful.

Trusting that God has a plan for your child, much like He did for Abraham, can bring you peace. Pray for the wisdom to guide them and the strength to let go when necessary. Trusting God with your child's growth and exploration is an act of faith, believing He will watch over them.

Finally, modeling independence yourself can be very impactful. Demonstrating that it's okay to pursue your own interests and spend time on personal growth shows your child the importance of independence and faith in God's plan.

Mom's Moments

Think about how you balance closeness and independence with your baby. How do you encourage their exploration while ensuring they feel your love and support? Write down a few ways to encourage your baby's indepen-

BIBLICAL TEACHINGS

dence while staying connected. Try one of these ideas this week and observe how it affects your baby's confidence and your bond.

Short Prayer

Dear God, help me balance loving closeness with encouraging my baby's independence. Grant me wisdom to guide them and faith to trust in Your plan. Amen.

8

CHOOSING HOW TO FEED YOUR BABY

___ / ___ / _____

> *"Boaz replied, 'I've been told all about what you have done for your mother-in-law since the death of your husband—how you left your father and mother and your homeland and came to live with a people you did not know before. May the Lord repay you for what you have done. May you be richly rewarded by the Lord, the God of Israel, under whose wings you have come to take refuge.'"*
>
> — RUTH 2:11-12

Have you ever found yourself awake in the middle of the night, rocking your baby, and wondering if you're making the right choices? One of the biggest decisions we face as new mothers is how to feed our little ones. *Should you breastfeed, use formula, or perhaps a combination of both?* Each option comes with its own challenges and benefits, and it can be difficult to know which path is best for your child and your family.

I remember those early days with my firstborn, feeling the pressure from all sides. Well-meaning friends and family offered advice, often conflicting, leaving me more confused than reassured. I had always imagined breastfeeding would be straightforward, but when I faced unexpected complications, my confidence wavered. Every feeding time became a battle between my expectations and reality, leading me to seek God's wisdom in my decision-making process.

During one particularly tough night, I found myself rereading the story of Ruth. Ruth's unwavering commitment to Naomi is a beautiful example of sacrificial love and provision. She left her own country, facing unknown challenges, to care for her mother-in-law. Like Ruth, we are called to provide for our children, often making sacrifices and difficult choices. Ruth sought God's refuge and was richly rewarded for her faith and dedication.

Reflecting on Ruth's journey, I realized that my decision on how to feed my baby was also a form of provision and sacrifice. When I chose to supplement with formula, I initially felt a twinge of guilt, fearing I was not doing enough. But through prayer and reflection, God reminded me that our choices, made with love and prayer, are honored by Him. It's not about the method but the heart and intention behind it. Feeding your baby, no matter how you do it, is an act of love and provision.

Remember, feeding your baby by breast or bottle manifests your love and care. You are meeting their needs as Ruth did for Naomi, and God sees your dedication. He honors the love and effort you pour into nurturing your little one. Your choice, made with prayerful consideration, is a testament to your commitment as a mother.

Mom's Moments

Reflect on your feeding journey. Write a letter to yourself about why you chose your feeding method, acknowledging the love and thoughtfulness behind your decision. Consider how God's guidance has shaped your choices, and thank Him for His presence in your journey.

Short Prayer

Dear God, guide me in feeding my baby with love and wisdom. Help me to find peace in my choices and trust in Your provision. Thank You for being with me every step of the way. Amen.

9

SOLVING COMMON FEEDING PROBLEMS

___ / ___ / _____

"She went away and did as Elijah had told her. So there was food every day for Elijah and for the woman and her family."

— 1 KINGS 17:15-16

Have you ever felt frustrated when feeding your baby didn't go as planned? Whether you're breastfeeding, using formula, or a mix of both, problems can come up that leave you feeling stressed and worried. I remember those times well, sitting with my baby and trying everything to get him to eat, feeling both helpless and determined.

Feeding challenges are something many new moms face, no matter how they choose to feed their babies. I recall one tough week when my baby wouldn't latch properly. Even though I had decided to breastfeed, it felt like I was failing. I tried different positions, asked friends for advice, and spent hours researching online, but nothing seemed to work.

During those difficult moments, I found comfort in the story of the widow feeding Elijah. Even when she had so little, her faith and trust reminded me of the importance of not giving up and believing in God's help. One night, after many unsuccessful attempts, I prayed for patience, guidance, and the strength to keep trying.

Things slowly started to get better. I talked to a lactation consultant who gave me helpful tips and support. I tried different nursing pillows, changed my techniques, and learned to better understand my baby's signals. Each small success felt like a big victory, reminding me to trust God.

Through this experience, I realized that feeding my baby wasn't just about the food—it was about building a bond and understanding each other. Just like the widow trusted God to provide, I learned to trust that God would help me through this challenge. The feeding problems didn't go away overnight, but they became easier to handle with patience and faith.

Mom's Moments

Think back to a time when you had a hard time feeding your baby. What did you learn from that experience? How did you keep going? Write a note to yourself with these thoughts and keep it somewhere special. Read your note whenever you face another challenge to remind yourself of your strength and perseverance.

Short Prayer

Dear God, give me patience and wisdom as I face feeding challenges with my baby. Help me trust in Your help and find joy in each small victory. Amen.

_____

_____

_____

_____

_____

_____

_____

10

STARTING SOLID FOODS

___ / ___ / _____

> *"Then Rebekah and her young women arose and rode on the camels and followed the man. Thus the servant took Rebekah and went his way."*
>
> — GENESIS 24:61 (ESV)

Have you ever experienced the mix of excitement and anxiety that comes with introducing solid foods to your baby? It's a significant milestone, filled with questions and hopes. Will they like it? Will it go smoothly? These moments, though small, are profound reminders of God's provision and care in our everyday lives.

I remember the day like it was yesterday. My friend Michelle, a first-time mom, was nervous about giving her six-month-old daughter, Bianca, her first taste of solid food. She had spent hours researching the best foods to start with, reading about baby-led weaning, and consulting other moms for advice. When the day finally came, she carefully prepared a small serving of mashed avocado. As she placed the spoon near Lily's lips, she silently prayed for this milestone to go smoothly.

Bianca's face was a canvas of pure amazement and wonder. She scrunched her nose, tasted the avocado, and then gave a wide, toothless grin. Michelle's heart swelled with gratitude. In that moment, she felt a deep connection to the story of Rebekah in the Bible, who provided nourishment and sustenance for her family. Just as Rebekah followed God's guidance, Michelle felt the Lord's presence guiding her through this new journey of motherhood.

Reflecting on this experience, I think about how introducing solid foods is not just about nutrition; it's a step towards independence and growth for our babies. It's a significant reminder of how God provides for us, nurturing us with both physical and spiritual food. Just as Rebekah trusted in God's plan and provision, we too can trust that He will guide us in caring for our little ones.

I remember my own experience vividly. When my son, Justin, was ready for his first solid meal, I chose sweet potatoes. The preparation was meticulous —I steamed and mashed the potatoes, making sure they were smooth and lump-free. The anticipation was palpable. Justin's reaction was a mix of curiosity and hesitation, followed by a delighted giggle as he tasted the sweetness. In that moment, I felt a profound sense of God's presence, reassuring me that every step of this journey was under His care.

Mom's Moment

Reflect on your baby's first experience with solid food. How did you see God's provision in that moment? Consider writing down your thoughts or sharing them with a fellow mom to encourage each other. This week, create a prayer of thanksgiving for God's provision in your baby's growth and share it with your baby during mealtime.

Short Prayer

Dear God, thank You for the joy of watching my baby grow and for guiding me in each new step of motherhood. Please help me to trust in Your provision and care. Amen.

MOM POWER: REFLECT & RENEW

DATE

S M T W T F S

REFLECTION

Moment of Strength

Think about a time when you felt strong as a mom. What happened, and how did you handle it?

_____
_____
_____

Source of Strength

Besides your faith, what helps you feel strong? (e.g., support from family, friends, or something else)

_____
_____
_____

PLANNING AHEAD

Handling Challenges

Think of a challenge you might face soon. Write down one thing you can do to stay strong during this time.

YOUR CHALLENGE:

YOUR PLAN:

CREATIVE ACTIVITY

Draw Your Strength

Draw or doodle something that represents strength to you. It could be a symbol, a person, or anything that comes to mind.

BIBLE VERSE REFLECTION

Exodus 2:3

Jochebed showed great courage in protecting her child. How does her story inspire you?

Your Reflection

_____

_____

_____

11

MAKING A SLEEP-FRIENDLY ENVIRONMENT

___ / ___ / _____

"She rises while it is yet night and provides food for her household and portions for her maidens."

— PROVERBS 31:15

Do you remember the first time you brought your baby home from the hospital? The joy, the excitement, and then the sleepless nights that followed? The delicate balance of caring for a newborn while managing your own exhaustion can feel overwhelming. Trust me, I've been there. Those early days often felt like a blur of feeding, changing, and rocking. However, one thing that made a significant difference for me was creating a sleep-friendly environment.

The Proverbs 31 woman is celebrated for her diligence and care. She rises early, ensuring her household is well cared for. This care extends to creating a restful environment for her family. I found inspiration in her example, realizing that making a calm and peaceful space for my baby could also bring peace to my own heart.

In my journey through motherhood, I discovered a few practical steps that helped. A consistent bedtime routine worked wonders—starting with a warm bath, then a gentle massage, and ending with a quiet story. I kept the room dark and cool, using white noise to drown out household sounds.

These steps created a predictable environment that helped signal to my baby that it was time to sleep.

But beyond the practical steps, there was something deeper. As I laid my baby down each night, I whispered a prayer. *"Lord, please watch over my little one tonight. Grant us peaceful rest."* Those moments of prayer weren't just about asking for a good night's sleep—they were about surrendering my worries and fears to God. I felt His presence in those quiet moments, reassuring me that I was not alone.

Mom's Moments

Tonight, as you prepare your baby for bed, dim the lights and play a soft lullaby. Whisper a prayer for peace and rest over your little one, and feel the calmness wash over you both.

Short Prayer

Dear God, Help me create a restful environment for my baby and me. Surround us with Your peace and comfort tonight. Amen.

12

HANDLING SLEEP REGRESSIONS & GROWTH SPURTS

___ / ___ / _____

> *"As she kept on praying to the Lord, Eli observed her mouth. Hannah was praying in her heart, and her lips were moving, but her voice was not heard."*
>
> — 1 SAMUEL 1:12-13

Have you ever felt the sting of exhaustion, your body craving rest while your baby seems determined to stay awake? Maybe it's 2 AM, and the gentle hum of the white noise machine is the only thing keeping you from feeling completely isolated. Sleep regressions and growth spurts can feel like never-ending battles, turning your peaceful nights into unpredictable challenges.

I vividly remember one night when my daughter went through a growth spurt. She woke up every hour, and nothing I did seemed to comfort her. As I rocked her in the dim light of her nursery, her cries echoing in the silence, I felt a wave of frustration and helplessness. Tears filled my eyes as I thought, *"Why won't she sleep? What am I doing wrong?"*

In moments like these, I often thought of Hannah from the Bible. Hannah, who longed for a child and prayed fervently to God, teaches us about the power of perseverance in prayer. Her silent prayers, full of heartfelt emotion, were a testament to her unwavering faith. In 1 Samuel 1:12-13, we see her praying in her heart, her lips moving but her voice unheard. It was her faith and persistence that eventually brought her peace.

As I sat in that rocking chair, I began to pray quietly. *"Lord, give me patience and strength. Help me to comfort my baby and bring her peace."* Just like Hannah, I poured out my heart to God, seeking His guidance and support. These silent, heartfelt prayers became my solace during the toughest nights.

With each passing hour, I noticed the little things—how my daughter's tiny fingers curled around mine, the softness of her cheek against my chest, the calm that eventually settled over her. These moments, though brief, reminded me of the preciousness of this time despite the exhaustion. They were whispers of God's grace in the chaos.

Mom's Moments

Create a "Blessings Jar." Each day, write down one small blessing or positive moment, no matter how small, and place it in the jar. On particularly tough nights, read through some of these notes to remind yourself of God's grace and the joy in motherhood.

Short Prayer

Dear God, grant me patience and strength through sleepless nights. Help my baby feel Your peace. Amen.

_____

_____

_____

_____

_____

_____

13

ADJUSTING YOUR SLEEP EXPECTATIONS

___ / ___ / _____

"But Mary treasured up all these things and pondered them in her heart."

— LUKE 2:19

How have your expectations about sleep changed since having a baby? Did you imagine blissful nights of rest, only to be in a perpetual state of exhaustion? I certainly did. I remember the stark difference between my pre-motherhood fantasies and the reality of sleepless nights, where my faith became a lifeline.

Before my first child, I was meticulous about my sleep. I had a bedtime routine that was practically sacred—chamomile tea, a good book, and lights out by 10 PM. I imagined that with some planning, my baby would seamlessly fit into this schedule. But once my little one arrived, I quickly learned that I could no longer command sleep. Those first few weeks were a blur of late-night feedings, diaper changes, and the mysterious cries that no swaddling could soothe. I was unprepared for how deeply fatigue could affect me, both physically and emotionally.

One particularly difficult night, I found myself in the nursery, rocking my baby back to sleep for what felt like the hundredth time. I was exhausted, frustrated, and on the verge of tears. As I sat there in the dim light, I remembered Mary, the mother of Jesus. Luke 2:19 tells us she *"treasured up all these things and pondered them in her heart."* Mary experienced uncertainty and probably sleepless nights, yet she found moments of reflection and peace amid chaos.

At that moment, I decided to change my perspective. Instead of focusing on my lack of sleep, I chose to see the beauty in the stillness of the night. I prayed for strength and patience and found solace in knowing that these sleepless nights were part of a sacred journey. My expectations shifted from seeking uninterrupted sleep to finding peace in the small, quiet moments with my baby.

I realized that faith could transform my exhaustion into a deeper connection with my child and God. Those nights when I felt I had nothing left to give, I leaned into prayer, seeking comfort and strength. I learned to appreciate the fleeting moments of calm, how my baby's tiny fingers would grasp mine, and the gentle rise and fall of their breath as they finally drifted off to sleep.

Mom's Moments

Create a cozy corner in your home where you can sit with your baby during those late-night feedings. Add a soft blanket, a comfortable chair, and a favorite devotional book or scripture cards. Use this space to find a moment of peace and prayer each night, making it a special time for you and your baby to connect with God.

Short Prayer

Dear God, grant me patience and strength through sleepless nights. Help me find peace in your presence and cherish these moments with my baby. Amen.

_____

_____

_____

14

HEALING AFTER GIVING BIRTH

___ / ___ / _____

> *"Then they moved on from Bethel. While they were still some distance from Ephrath, Rachel began to give birth and had great difficulty. And as she was having great difficulty in childbirth, the midwife said to her, 'Don't despair, for you have another son.'"*
>
> — GENESIS 35:16-17

Approximately 90% of women experience some form of physical complication during childbirth, whether minor or major. These challenges can range from unexpected cesarean sections to prolonged labor and significant postpartum recovery periods. Each mother's journey of healing is unique, marked by both struggles and triumphs.

A Bible story that resonates with this is the story of Rachel, the beloved wife of Jacob, who endured a particularly arduous labor. Her story is a poignant one, marked by both intense pain and the promise of new life. The midwife's words to Rachel, *"Don't despair, for you have another son,"* offer a glimmer of hope amidst her suffering. Rachel's experience is a powerful reminder of the challenges and the miraculous nature of childbirth.

For many new mothers, the days following birth can be filled with unexpected challenges. I remember my own recovery after my first child was born. The exhaustion was unlike anything I had ever experienced. My body ached in ways I hadn't anticipated, and sleep seemed like a distant memory. Yet, in those quiet moments of nursing my baby and feeling the rhythm of her breathing, I found a profound sense of peace and purpose. It was in these intimate moments that I felt God's hand guiding me, providing the strength I needed to care for my newborn and heal.

Maybe you struggled with the physical pain of a C-section or the emotional rollercoaster of postpartum depression. Perhaps you found unexpected joy in the simplicity of holding your baby close, marveling at their tiny fingers and toes. Each scar, each sleepless night, each moment of doubt and joy is a testament to your strength and resilience. And through it all, God is with you, just as He was with Rachel.

Mom's Moments

Take a moment to create a "healing journal." Write down your recovery experiences, noting both the challenges and the moments of joy. Include prayers, Bible verses, and reflections on how you've seen God's hand in your healing process. Share a page from your journal with a close friend or fellow mom to encourage and uplift one another.

Short Prayer

Dear God, thank You for guiding me through the healing process after giving birth. Help me to see Your hand in my journey and find strength in Your presence. Amen.

_____

_____

_____

_____

15

STARTING TO EXERCISE AGAIN

___ / ___ / _____

"I can do all things through Christ who strengthens me."

— PHILIPPIANS 4:13

As new moms, our lives are filled with so many changes, finding time for ourselves can seem impossible. I remember those early days well—when my body felt foreign, and the idea of exercise felt like a distant dream.

In those overwhelming moments, I found inspiration in the story of the woman with the issue of blood. For twelve long years, she endured suffering and isolation, yet she never lost hope. Her faith drove her to push through the crowd just to touch the hem of Jesus' cloak, believing in the possibility of healing. And Jesus, recognizing her faith, granted her the healing she sought.

Her story became a powerful metaphor for my own journey. I realized that, like her, I needed to reach out in faith, trusting that God cared about every aspect of my life, including my physical well-being. I started small, just as she did. My first steps were tentative—short walks around the block with my baby in a stroller. These walks weren't just physical exercise; they became a sanctuary of peace and prayer, moments where I could breathe and connect with God amidst the chaos.

I vividly recall one afternoon when, feeling particularly drained, I hesitated to go out. But I bundled up my baby and stepped outside, whispering a prayer for strength. As I walked, the fresh air cleared my mind, and a sense of calm washed over me. It was in those simple, faithful steps that I found not just physical strength, but a spiritual renewal. Each walk became a testament to God's presence in my journey, reminding me that I was never alone.

Gradually, these small steps turned into a routine. I began to incorporate more structured exercises, always mindful to listen to my body and to invite God into my efforts. The transformation wasn't just physical; it was holistic. I felt more energized, more patient, and more equipped to handle the demands of motherhood.

Mom's Moments

Today, try a simple, joyful exercise with your baby. Play a game of "airplane" where you gently lift your baby up while lying on your back. This playful activity strengthens your core and creates joyful bonding moments. As you do this, thank God for the gift of your child and the strength He gives you.

Short Prayer

Dear God, grant me the strength and motivation to care for my body, so I can be the best mother for my child. Amen.

_____

_____

_____

_____

_____

_____

16

EATING WELL FOR ENERGY & RECOVERY

___ / ___ / _____

> *"So Ruth gleaned in the field until evening. Then she threshed the barley she had gathered, and it amounted to about an ephah."*
>
> — RUTH 2:17

Nearly 60% of new mothers experience postpartum fatigue, a condition worsen by the physical demands of caring for a newborn. With sleepless nights and constant feedings, your body and mind are stretched thin. But have you considered how vital proper nourishment is in this season? Your body needs fuel, not just to function, but to thrive.

This is something similar to the story of Ruth, who spent long days gleaning in the fields. Her hard work was not just about survival, but about trusting God's provision. She gathered grain diligently, knowing it was essential for her and Naomi's sustenance. As a new mom, you too must gather your *"grain"*—the nutritious foods that will help you recover and keep your energy up.

It's a typical morning, and your baby has been up multiple times through the night. You're running on little sleep, and breakfast feels like an insurmountable task. You reach for something quick and easy—a piece of toast or a cup of coffee. But what if, instead, you took a few extra minutes to prepare a smoothie packed with spinach, berries, and a scoop of protein powder? This small change can set a positive tone for your day, providing the energy you need to care for your little one.

Maybe lunchtime arrives, and you're tempted to grab a processed snack. Instead, consider a hearty bowl of quinoa salad with veggies and lean protein. Each meal you choose with intention is a step toward better health and energy. It's not just about eating; it's about honoring your body as a temple of the Holy Spirit and recognizing that these nourishing foods are God's provision for you.

Mom's Moments

Create a weekly meal plan focused on nutritious meals and snacks. Include colorful fruits, vegetables, lean proteins, and whole grains. Track how these changes make you feel over the week, and share your experience with another new mom for encouragement.

Short Prayer

Dear God, thank You for providing the nourishment I need to care for my baby. Help me make healthy choices to sustain my energy and aid my recovery. Amen.

17

FINDING TIME FOR SELF-CARE

___ / ___ / _____

"She had a sister called Mary, who sat at the Lord's feet listening to what he said."

— LUKE 10:39

Have you ever felt like you're losing yourself in the chaos of motherhood? I certainly have. I remember one particular day when I was at my wit's end. My youngest had colic and screamed for hours, my toddler decided that everything was a reason for a meltdown, and the older kids needed help with their homework. By the time my husband came home, I was exhausted, frazzled, and feeling like a shadow of myself. It seemed impossible to find a moment to breathe, let alone spend time with God.

In the midst of that overwhelming season, I was reminded of the story of Mary and Martha. Martha was busy with the tasks of the household, while Mary chose to sit at Jesus' feet and listen to His words. Initially, I identified with Martha—how could Mary just sit there when there was so much to do? But the more I pondered this story, the more I realized that Mary's choice wasn't about neglecting her responsibilities but about prioritizing her spiritual well-being. She knew that to truly serve others, she first needed to be filled by Jesus' presence.

Inspired by Mary, I realized I needed to find my own moments to sit at Jesus' feet. But how could I do that with the constant demands of motherhood? I started to get creative. During my baby's nap, instead of rushing to finish chores, I began to take a few minutes for myself. I would brew a cup of tea, sit by the window, and open my Bible or a devotional book. Sometimes, I would just sit in silence, breathing deeply, and feeling God's presence wash over me.

This small act of self-care transformed my days. It wasn't about neglecting my family but about making sure I was spiritually and emotionally nourished. I found that when I took time to recharge, I became a more patient and joyful mother. My spiritual well-being improved, and I felt more connected to God. Those few minutes of peace gave me the strength to face the demands of motherhood with a renewed spirit.

Mom's Moments

Create a "sanctuary" spot in your home. It could be a cozy chair by the window or a corner of your bedroom. Make it a place where you can retreat for a few minutes each day to read a verse, pray, or simply breathe deeply. Use this space to reconnect with God and yourself. Another idea is to combine self-care with your baby's routine, like praying or listening to worship music during feeding times or walks.

Short Prayer

Dear God, help me carve out moments of peace amidst the chaos of motherhood. Replenish my spirit so I can care for my baby with love and patience. Amen.

_____

_____

_____

_____

18

KNOWING THE DIFFERENCE BETWEEN BABY BLUES & DEPRESSION

___ / ___ / _____

> *"Then the women said to Naomi, 'Blessed be the Lord, who has not left you this day without a redeemer, and may his name be renowned in Israel! He shall be to you a restorer of life and a nourisher of your old age, for your daughter-in-law who loves you, who is more to you than seven sons, has given birth to him.'"*
>
> — RUTH 4:14-15

Have you ever felt like the joy of motherhood is overshadowed by a cloud you can't shake? It's a feeling many new moms experience but seldom talk about. Leni had always dreamed of being a mother. When she finally held her newborn daughter, Rose, in her arms, she felt a joy she had never known. The nursery was ready, filled with pastel colors and soft toys. Friends and family showered her with congratulations and gifts, and her husband was a constant support. Yet, despite the love and happiness that surrounded her, Leni felt an unexpected and overwhelming sadness creeping in.

The first few days at home were a blur of diaper changes, feedings, and sleepless nights. Leni attributed her tearfulness and anxiety to exhaustion. *"It's just the baby blues,"* she told herself, a term she had heard tossed around in prenatal classes. But weeks went by, and instead of feeling better, Leni felt worse. She found herself crying uncontrollably, feeling isolated even in the company of loved ones, and struggling with a heavy sense of guilt for not feeling the joy she had expected.

Leni's experience echoes the story of Naomi from the Bible. Naomi had lost her husband and sons, and her grief was so profound that she asked to be called Mara, which means *"bitter."* Naomi felt abandoned and lost, much like Sarah did. But God had a plan for Naomi, restoring her joy through the birth of her grandson, Obed. This story resonated deeply with Leni.

One particularly difficult afternoon, Leni sat in the nursery rocking Rose, tears streaming down her face. Her husband found her there and gently took her hand. *"We need to talk to someone,"* he said softly. That evening, they prayed together, seeking God's guidance and strength. Leni felt a small flicker of hope as she remembered Naomi's transformation from bitterness to joy. She realized that acknowledging her struggle was the first step towards healing.

Leni reached out to her doctor, who diagnosed her with postpartum depression. It was a relief to put a name to her feelings and to know that she wasn't alone. With professional help, the support of her husband, and the prayers of her community, Leni began to see a light at the end of the tunnel. She joined a local support group for new mothers and found comfort in sharing her story and hearing others'. Slowly, she started to bond more with Lily and enjoy the little moments that motherhood brought.

Mom's Moments

Create a small gratitude journal. Each day, write down three things you are thankful for, no matter how small. Then, reach out to another new mom and share your entries. This can foster a sense of community and support.

Short Prayer

Dear God, help me to recognize my feelings and give me the strength to seek help when needed. Bless my baby and me with Your peace and guidance. Amen.

19

STAYING PRESENT & MINDFUL

___ / ___ / _____

"But his mother treasured all these things in her heart."

— LUKE 2:51

Many new mothers feel overwhelmed by the daily demands of caring for their babies. The constant cycle of feedings, diaper changes, and sleepless nights can make it hard to stay present and mindful. However, amidst this whirlwind, there are precious moments waiting to be cherished.

Mary, the mother of Jesus, treasured moments with her child even in the midst of her busy life. This reminds us that, like Mary, we can find peace and presence in our daily lives. I remember an afternoon when my baby had been fussy all day, and nothing seemed to soothe him. The house was a mess, my to-do list was long, and my patience was wearing thin.

As I sat in the rocking chair, cradling my baby close, I felt a wave of exhaustion and frustration wash over me. Tears welled up in my eyes, and I silently prayed for strength. At that moment, I felt a tiny hand grasp my finger. I looked down to see my baby's eyes, full of trust, staring back at me. A sense of calm enveloped me, and I was reminded of the preciousness of this fleeting time.

In these quiet, intimate moments, I felt God's presence most profoundly. Being present isn't about having everything under control or accomplishing all my tasks. It's about embracing the here and now, finding joy in the little things, and recognizing the divine in the mundane. My baby's gentle breathing, the softness of his skin, and the sweet, innocent coos were all reminders of God's love and grace.

One Saturday morning, my husband took on the yard work, giving me a few hours of quiet inside. Instead of catching up on chores, I decided to simply be with my baby. We lay on a blanket in the living room, surrounded by soft toys and the sound of birds outside. I watched as my baby discovered his feet, and we laughed together. In those moments, I felt a profound connection to him and to God.

Mom's Moments

Set aside a specific time each day to have a "mindfulness moment" with your baby. Whether it's during feeding, bath time, or a quiet cuddle, focus entirely on your baby, noticing every detail and feeling the connection. Journal about these moments and how they bring you closer to God.

Short Prayer

Dear God, help me to stay present and mindful, treasuring each moment with my baby as a gift from You. Amen.

_____

_____

_____

_____

_____

20

MANAGING STRESS IN HEALTHY WAYS

___ / ___ / _____

"Martha, Martha," the Lord answered, "you are worried and upset about many things, but few things are needed—or indeed only one. Mary has chosen what is better, and it will not be taken away from her."

— LUKE 10:41-42

How do you cope with stress and maintain mental health as a new mom? The demands are endless, and the pressures seem insurmountable. Yet, amidst the whirlwind, there lies a gentle whisper, guiding you towards peace.

Imagine Martha in the Bible, bustling around, trying to get everything perfect for her guests. She was stressed and overwhelmed, much like you might feel when trying to balance all your new responsibilities. Martha was so caught up in the busyness that she forgot the most important thing—being present with Jesus.

In our modern lives, it's easy to feel like Martha. The baby needs feeding, the laundry is piling up, and you haven't had a moment to yourself in days. The stress can become all-consuming. But in the midst of this chaos, Jesus' words to Martha offer a lifeline: focus on what truly matters.

One evening, after a particularly exhausting day, I found myself sitting on the nursery floor, surrounded by toys and baby clothes. I felt overwhelmed and on the verge of tears. At that moment, I remembered Martha and her encounter with Jesus. I closed my eyes, took a deep breath, and prayed. I asked God to help me focus on what was truly important and to find peace amidst the chaos.

Surprisingly, that simple prayer brought a sense of calm over me. I realized that, like Mary, I needed to take time to sit at Jesus' feet, even if just for a few minutes each day. Those moments of quiet reflection and prayer became my sanctuary, helping me to reset and find balance.

Stress is an inevitable part of motherhood, but how we manage it makes all the difference. Instead of trying to do everything perfectly, give yourself grace. Prioritize time with God, and let His peace wash over you. It's okay to leave some things undone and focus on what truly matters—your relationship with Him and your baby.

Mom's Moments

Find a quiet corner today and spend five minutes in prayer or meditation, focusing on God's presence and releasing your worries to Him.

Short Prayer

Dear God, in my moments of stress, help me find peace in Your presence. Guide me to prioritize what truly matters. Amen.

_____

_____

_____

_____

_____

21

ASKING FOR HELP WHEN YOU NEED IT

___ / ___ / _____

> *"Jesus answered, 'Everyone who drinks this water will be thirsty again, but whoever drinks the water I give them will never thirst. Indeed, the water I give them will become in them a spring of water welling up to eternal life.'"*
>
> — JOHN 4:13-14

Most new mothers experience feelings of being overwhelmed and isolated. Caring for a newborn, managing a household, and maintaining emotional well-being can create immense stress. I remember one afternoon when, as my baby napped, I felt an overwhelming emptiness. It was then I realized I needed more than just rest—I needed spiritual renewal and support.

I thought of the woman at the well, who sought water but found much more in her encounter with Jesus. She was burdened by her past, yet Jesus offered her living water—eternal life and a relationship with God that satisfies our deepest needs. As a new mother, I often felt like I was drawing from an empty well, trying to meet everyone's needs while neglecting my own.

We often believe we must carry the burdens of motherhood alone, but Jesus' encounter at the well shows us the importance of seeking help. When I shared my struggles with a friend, her prayers and reminders of God's love gave me the relief I needed. In sharing my burdens, I found the living water Jesus spoke of—a source of strength and renewal.

Consider the areas in your life where you feel overwhelmed—whether it's sleepless nights or the pressure to be the perfect mother. Know that asking for help is not a sign of weakness; it's an invitation for God to work through others. Even Jesus sought help in His darkest hours.

Help often comes in unexpected ways. One day, a neighbor offered to watch my baby for a couple of hours. Initially hesitant, I accepted, and it allowed me to recharge and become a better mother. This reminded me that God provides support through others when we open ourselves to it.

Mom's Moments

Today, take a moment to reflect on where you need help. Write down one area where you feel overwhelmed and make a plan to reach out to someone you trust for support.

Short Prayer

Dear God, help me to recognize when I need help and to have the courage to ask for it. Surround me with supportive people who can remind me of Your love and grace. Amen.

22

APPRECIATING YOUR BODY AFTER CHILDBIRTH

___ / ___ / _____

"Sarah became pregnant and bore a son to Abraham in his old age, at the very time God had promised him."

— GENESIS 21:2

A lot of new mothers struggle with body image issues post-pregnancy. This highlights a common reality: the journey through pregnancy and childbirth profoundly changes your body. But with all the changes, have you taken a moment to appreciate the amazing things your body has done?

Think about Sarah, who gave birth in her old age. Despite the improbability, her body nurtured and brought forth life because of God's promise. Like Sarah, your body has been a vessel of God's miraculous work, nurturing and bringing forth new life. Sarah's story is not just about a miraculous birth; it's about the faith and strength that carried her through the process. Her body, despite its limitations and age, became a testament to God's power and promise.

Your journey is similar. Each stretch mark, curve, and scar tells a story of strength, resilience, and divine craftsmanship. The physical changes you see are not flaws but badges of honor that reflect the incredible task your body has performed. Every sleepless night, every bout of morning sickness, and every contraction has brought you closer to the miracle of life.

Think about the amazing journey your body went through to create and nurture life. From the moment you conceived, your body turned into a safe haven, giving your baby everything it needed to grow and develop. This incredible transformation shows God's wonderful design and purpose. Just like Sarah's body was specially made to fulfill God's promise to her, your body was perfectly designed with the strength and ability to bring new life into the world.

It's easy to focus on what you perceive as imperfections, especially in a world that often emphasizes unrealistic standards of beauty. But take a moment to see yourself through God's eyes. He sees the beauty in your sacrifice, the strength in your perseverance, and the miracle in your transformation. Your body is a living testament to His love and power.

Mom's Moments

Treat yourself to a spa day at home. Light some candles, play your favorite worship music, and give your body the pampering it deserves. As you do, reflect on each part of your body and the role it played in bringing your baby into the world. Write a letter to yourself, celebrating the journey and the strength you've shown.

Short Prayer

Dear God, thank You for the incredible strength and resilience You've designed in my body. Help me to see its beauty and appreciate the miracle it has accomplished. Amen.

_____

_____

_____

23

UNEXPECTED BODY CHANGES POST-BIRTH

___ / ___ / _____

> *"After these days his wife Elizabeth conceived, and for five months she kept herself hidden, saying, 'Thus the Lord has done for me in the days when he looked on me, to take away my reproach among people.'"*
>
> — LUKE 1:24-25 (ESV)

From stretch marks to unexpected weight retention, or even changes in hair and skin, the post-birth body often feels like unfamiliar territory. You pull on your favorite jeans that used to fit perfectly, but now they feel different. The frustration can be overwhelming, making you question your worth and beauty.

That reminds me of Elizabeth, who experienced an unexpected and miraculous pregnancy later in life. While scripture doesn't detail her physical experiences, we can infer that her body went through significant changes. She kept herself hidden for five months, possibly adjusting to the extraordinary changes happening within her. Elizabeth's story reminds us that even when changes are challenging, they are part of God's plan.

Post-birth changes are a common experience. One mother shared how her feet grew a size larger and never returned to their original size. Another noticed that her hair, once thick and lustrous, began to shed significantly. These changes, though unexpected, are natural responses to the incredible journey of bringing new life into the world.

I recall a time after my third child was born when I felt overwhelmed by the changes in my body. My favorite clothes no longer fit, and my energy levels were lower than before. I found myself feeling less confident and more critical of my appearance. But it was during these moments of self-doubt that I turned to prayer and reflection, seeking strength and reassurance from God. I realized that these changes were marks of the miraculous gift of life. Each stretch mark, each new curve, was a testament to the incredible feat my body accomplished.

One evening, as I sat feeding my baby, I thought about how Elizabeth might have felt during her pregnancy. She, too, must have faced physical and emotional changes, yet she embraced them with faith. Her story encouraged me to see my own body through a lens of gratitude rather than criticism. I began to appreciate the changes as evidence of God's work in my life.

Talking to other new moms, I found that many of them shared similar feelings. One friend mentioned how she felt a profound sense of loss over her pre-baby body. Another spoke about the struggle with postpartum depression and how it affected her perception of herself. These conversations were a reminder that we are not alone in our experiences. Sharing our stories and supporting each other can make a significant difference.

Mom's Moments

Spend some time doing gentle stretches or yoga. As you move, focus on each part of your body and the incredible work it has done. Breathe deeply and thank God for the strength and resilience He has given you.

Short Prayer

Dear God, help me to embrace and celebrate the changes in my body, understanding they are signs of the incredible life I've brought into the world. Amen.

MOM POWER: REFLECT & RENEW

DATE

S M T W T F S

REFLECTION

Experiencing Exhaustion

Share a time when you felt particularly exhausted as a new mom. What emotions did you experience, and how did you seek support or comfort?

_____
_____
_____

Finding Rest in Faith

Reflect on how your faith has helped you find rest and peace during sleepless nights. What prayers or practices have been particularly comforting?

_____
_____
_____

PLANNING AHEAD

Adjusting Sleep Expectations

How have your expectations about sleep changed since becoming a mom? Write down one way you can adjust your mindset to be more compassionate towards yourself during these times.

YOUR PLAN:

CREATIVE ACTIVITY
Create a Relaxing Ritual

Design a simple nighttime ritual for yourself that helps you wind down. It could include reading a devotional, listening to soft music, or praying. How does this ritual help you connect with God and find peace?

BIBLE VERSE REFLECTION

Luke 2:19
But Mary treasured up all these things and pondered them in her heart.

Your Reflection

THE POWER OF ENCOURAGEMENT

"Let us consider how we may spur one another on toward love and good deeds."

— HEBREWS 10:24

Being a new mom is an amazing journey, full of ups and downs, love, and learning. If this devotional has brought you comfort, strength, or joy, we have a special request for you.

Would you help someone you've never met, even if you never got credit for it?

Who is this person, you ask? They are like you. Or, at least, like you used to be. Less experienced, seeking guidance, and looking for a way to connect with God through the challenges of motherhood.

Our mission is to make the journey of new motherhood a spiritually enriching experience for every mom. Everything we do stems from that mission. And, the only way for us to accomplish that mission is by reaching...well...everyone.

This is where you come in. Most people do, in fact, judge a book by its cover (and its reviews). So here's my ask on behalf of a struggling new mom you've never met:

Please help that new mom by leaving this book a review.

Your gift costs no money and less than 60 seconds to make real, but it can change a fellow mom's life forever. Your review could help...

...one more mom finds peace during sleepless nights.

...one more woman feels supported and less alone.

...one more reader discovers strength in God's love.

...one more person finds joy in the little moments with her baby.

...one more mother connects with her faith more deeply.

To get that 'feel good' feeling and help this person for real, all you have to do is leave a review. Simply **scan the QR code below:**

If you feel good about helping a faceless new mom, you are our kind of person. Welcome to the club. You're one of us.

Thank you from the bottom of our hearts. Now, back to our regularly scheduled programming.

Your biggest fan,

Biblical Teachings

Relationship & IDENTITY

24

SHARING PARENTING DUTIES

___ / ___ / _____

"Priscilla and Aquila invited him to their home and explained to him the way of God more adequately."

— ACTS 18:26

Have you ever wondered how some couples seem to navigate the tumultuous waters of parenting with such grace and unity? How do they maintain a partnership that is both faith-centered and balanced in responsibilities? Let's talk about Priscilla and Aquila, a couple whose deep devotion to God was matched by their remarkable teamwork, both in their ministry and everyday lives.

They were tentmakers by trade, but their real passion lay in their ministry. Together, they taught, hosted, and nurtured the early Christian community. Their story in Acts 18:26 shows us a beautiful example of a couple who worked hand in hand, complementing each other's strengths and covering each other's weaknesses. They didn't just share a home or a job; they shared a mission, a life of purpose rooted deeply in their faith.

One evening, as the sun set over their humble workshop, Priscilla and Aquila welcomed Apollos, a learned man with a fervent spirit but limited understanding of the Gospel. With patience and unity, they invited him into their home and shared the complete story of Jesus. It wasn't just the words they spoke, but the harmony in their partnership that made a lasting impact on Apollos.

In our modern context, sharing parenting duties can often feel overwhelming, especially when both partners have demanding roles outside the home. But imagine if we approached parenting as Priscilla and Aquila approached their ministry – as a united front, each bringing their unique gifts to the table, supporting and uplifting each other. This requires open communication, a willingness to serve one another, and a shared commitment to keep Christ at the center of your partnership.

Think about how you and your partner can divide parenting duties in a way that reflects your shared values and strengths. Perhaps one of you is naturally more patient and can handle bedtime routines, while the other enjoys cooking and can take charge of meal preparations. The key is not to strive for a perfect 50/50 split but to seek balance and support in a way that feels right for your family.

When my husband and I had our first child, we quickly realized that our preconceived notions of parenting roles were less important than finding a rhythm that worked for us. I was always better at soothing our baby to sleep, while my husband had a knack for making bath time fun. We learned to appreciate each other's strengths and lean into them, making our partnership stronger and our home more peaceful.

There were times, of course, when exhaustion led to frustration. We had to remind ourselves to communicate openly and to approach our duties with a servant's heart. On one particularly trying night, when our baby had colic, I remember my husband taking over with a simple, *"You rest, I've got this."* In that moment, I felt such gratitude for his support and partnership. It was a tangible expression of love and a reminder that we were in this together.

For many of us, juggling work, home, and baby care can sometimes lead to feelings of isolation or resentment. It's easy to fall into the trap of keeping score – who changed more diapers, who woke up more times at night. But focusing on what each of you can bring to the partnership, rather than what you're owed, can transform the experience of parenting into one of shared joy and mutual support.

BIBLICAL TEACHINGS

Mom's Moments

Try setting aside a weekly "Parenting Partnership" meeting with your spouse. Use this time to discuss what's working well, what needs adjustment, and how you can better support each other. End each meeting with a prayer, asking for God's guidance and blessing on your partnership.

Short Prayer

Dear God, help us to work together in unity, sharing our strengths and supporting each other as we raise our baby. Guide us to keep You at the center of our partnership. Amen.

_____
_____
_____
_____
_____
_____
_____
_____
_____
_____
_____
_____
_____
_____

25

STAYING CLOSE DESPITE BEING TIRED

___ / ___ / _____

> "So God said to Abraham, 'Do not be so distressed about the boy and your slave woman. Listen to whatever Sarah tells you, because it is through Isaac that your offspring will be reckoned.'"
>
> — GENESIS 21:12

Have you ever felt so exhausted that the thought of connecting with your partner feels like just another item on an already overwhelming to-do list? As new mothers, our days are filled with endless demands, from sleepless nights to the constant care our little ones require. It's easy to feel disconnected from our partners when we're running on empty. But how do we stay close despite the exhaustion?

I remember a time when my husband and I were in the thick of it. Our newborn was colicky, and sleep was a rare commodity. We barely had the energy to have a conversation, let alone connect on a deeper level. One evening, after a particularly grueling day, I found myself snapping at him over something trivial. The exhaustion was taking its toll on both of us, and it was affecting our relationship.

That night, after we finally got our baby to sleep, we sat down together in the quiet of our living room. We turned to the story of Sarah and Abraham, a partnership marked by its own set of trials and triumphs. Despite the challenges they faced, they leaned on their faith and each other. Sarah and Abraham's journey reminded us that we are not alone in our struggles and that God's guidance is always available to us.

We decided to make a commitment to reconnect daily, even if it was just for a few minutes. We prayed together, asking God to give us the strength and patience we needed to nurture our relationship as well as our baby. Those moments of prayer and reflection became a lifeline, sustaining us through the exhaustion.

Our nightly routine began to change. Instead of zoning out in front of the TV or retreating into our phones, we made a conscious effort to talk, to share our feelings and thoughts about the day. Sometimes, we read a passage from the Bible and reflected on it together. Other times, we simply sat in silence, holding hands, finding comfort in each other's presence.

It wasn't always easy. There were nights when we were too tired to do more than exchange a few words. But even in those moments, we felt a sense of unity and peace, knowing that we were in this together, guided by our faith.

We also learned to appreciate the small acts of kindness and support that we offered each other throughout the day. Whether it was my husband taking over a late-night feeding so I could get a bit more sleep or me making his favorite breakfast despite my fatigue, these gestures became a language of love that strengthened our bond.

Reflecting on Sarah and Abraham's story, we realized that their partnership was not just about enduring hardships together but also about celebrating the blessings and joys that God bestowed upon them. We began to see our challenges as opportunities to grow closer, to support each other, and to deepen our faith.

Mom's Moments

Create a "connection jar" with your partner. Write down simple activities on small pieces of paper that you can do together, like taking a short walk, sharing a favorite scripture, or enjoying a cup of tea after the baby is asleep. Each day, draw an activity from the jar and spend that time reconnecting.

Short Prayer

Dear God, give us the strength to stay connected and the patience to support each other through our exhaustion. Help us to find joy and love in the small moments. Amen.

26

SUPPORTING EACH OTHER'S PARENTING STYLES

___ / ___ / _____

"Then Elkanah her husband said to her, 'Hannah, why do you weep? Why do you not eat? And why is your heart grieved? Am I not better to you than ten sons?'"

— 1 SAMUEL 1:8 (NKJV)

Supporting your partner's parenting style, especially when it clashes with your own, can be challenging. Parenting, like any other journey in life, is filled with opportunities for growth and demands a delicate balance of mutual respect, understanding, and unwavering faith. The story of Hannah and Elkanah illustrates the essence of supporting one another through different perspectives.

Hannah was deeply distressed over her inability to conceive a child, and her sorrow consumed her. Elkanah, her loving husband, offered her comfort and support despite not fully understanding the depth of her grief. His words to Hannah, while seemingly simple, were filled with compassion and an attempt to soothe her troubled heart. He recognized her pain and stood by her, providing emotional support and love.

In our modern lives, we often face similar situations in our parenting journey. You and your partner might have differing views on various aspects of raising your child – from discipline methods to daily routines. These differences can sometimes lead to misunderstandings and tension. However, just as Elkanah supported Hannah, you can support your partner by embracing their unique parenting style and recognizing the strengths it brings to your family.

For instance, imagine a scenario where you prefer a structured approach to bedtime routines while your partner enjoys a more relaxed and spontaneous method. Instead of seeing this as a conflict, view it as an opportunity to blend the best of both worlds. The structure you provide offers stability and predictability, while your partner's spontaneity can make bedtime more enjoyable and less stressful for your child. By working together and appreciating each other's methods, you create a balanced environment that caters to your child's diverse needs.

Consider the ways Elkanah demonstrated his support. He did not demand that Hannah suppress her feelings or adopt his perspective. Instead, he offered a listening ear and comforting presence. This teaches us the importance of empathy and active listening in our relationships. When your partner expresses their parenting ideas or concerns, listen with an open heart and mind. Validate their feelings and acknowledge their efforts, even if you don't always agree.

Mom's Moments

Plan a "Parent Swap Day." For one day, try adopting your partner's parenting style in a particular activity, whether it's bedtime, playtime, or mealtime. Notice how your child responds and share your experiences with each other at the end of the day. This exercise can build empathy and appreciation for each other's approaches.

Short Prayer

Dear God, grant me patience and understanding to support my partner's parenting style with love and grace. Amen.

27

MAKING TIME FOR EACH OTHER

___ / ___ / _____

> *"So Joseph also went up from the town of Nazareth in Galilee to Judea, to Bethlehem the town of David, because he belonged to the house and line of David. He went there to register with Mary, who was pledged to be married to him and was expecting a child."*
>
> — LUKE 2:4-5

Staying connected with your partner can be incredibly challenging when it feels like your baby has taken over every moment of your lives. I remember those early days when my husband and I were so sleep-deprived and busy with our newborn that we barely had time to say more than a few words to each other. It felt like we were living parallel lives under the same roof, just trying to get through each day.

Mary and Joseph's journey to Bethlehem and their experience as new parents to Jesus provide a beautiful example of partnership and teamwork. They faced enormous challenges together, from traveling long distances while Mary was heavily pregnant to finding a place to stay and eventually welcoming their child in a humble stable. Despite the hardships, their unity and faith in God helped them navigate the challenges of parenthood.

For us, finding time to reconnect required intentional effort. We had to learn to cherish the small moments, turning them into opportunities for meaningful connection. A simple coffee break while the baby napped, a shared chore in the kitchen, or even a quiet walk around the block became precious times for us to talk, laugh, and pray together. Prayer, in particular, became a cornerstone of our reconnection. It was in those moments of shared prayer that we found peace, strength, and a deeper bond. Inviting God into our relationship helped us to prioritize each other and remind us of the love that initially brought us together.

In those early months, we realized the importance of setting aside intentional time for each other, no matter how brief. Sometimes, it was as simple as sitting on the porch after the baby had gone to bed, sharing our thoughts and dreams. Other times, it involved planning a special date night at home, with the baby monitor close by, and enjoying a homemade dinner together. These moments allowed us to remember why we fell in love in the first place and reinforced our commitment to each other.

We also found that incorporating prayer into our daily routine was transformative. Praying together not only brought us closer to God but also to each other. It created a space for us to express our gratitude, our worries, and our hopes, fostering a deeper emotional and spiritual connection. We would often end our days by praying together, asking for guidance and strength to navigate the challenges of parenthood and to continue to grow in our love for one another.

Additionally, involving our baby in our prayer time became a special family tradition. We would hold our baby and pray over them, thanking God for the gift of our child and asking for His protection and guidance. This practice not only strengthened our bond as a couple but also as a family unit, creating a foundation of faith and love that we hoped to pass on to our child.

Mom's Moments

Plan a mini date night at home. Once the baby is asleep, prepare a simple dessert or a favorite snack, light a candle, and spend 15 minutes just talking and praying together. Share your highs and lows of the day, and remind each other of the love that brought you together.

Short Prayer

Dear God, help us find moments to connect and strengthen our bond. Guide us to support each other and keep our love strong amidst the demands of parenthood. Amen.

28

KEEPING YOUR HOBBIES ALIVE

___ / ___ / _____

> *"One of those listening was a woman from the city of Thyatira named Lydia, a dealer in purple cloth. She was a worshiper of God. The Lord opened her heart to respond to Paul's message. When she and the members of her household were baptized, she invited us to her home."*
>
> — ACTS 16:14-15

Hobbies and activities that once brought joy can often seem like distant memories amidst the packed days of feeding, diaper changes, and the quest for a moment of sleep. As a mom, it's easy to let interests fall by the wayside. However, Lydia, a woman from the Bible, shows us it's possible to keep our passions alive even in the busiest of times.

Lydia was a successful businesswoman, selling purple cloth, which was a luxurious item back then. Despite her busy schedule, she made time for her faith. When Paul preached in her city, she listened carefully and felt moved by his words. Her faith wasn't just a private affair—it spilled over into her household, and she even opened her home to Paul and his companions.

Imagine Lydia's daily life—managing a thriving business and running a household. Yet, she didn't let these responsibilities consume her completely.

Lydia found a way to blend her faith and her interests, turning her home into a place of both business and ministry. Her story teaches us that our hobbies don't have to disappear just because we're moms. They can fit into our lives in new and meaningful ways.

Think about Andrea, a new mom who loved gardening before her baby arrived. After becoming a mom, she struggled to find time for her plants. Her days were filled with the endless cycle of feeding, changing, and trying to get her baby to sleep. One afternoon, feeling particularly drained, she decided to take her baby outside in a carrier and spend just ten minutes in her garden. As she pulled weeds and watered her plants, she felt a wave of peace and happiness wash over her.

Those few minutes became her lifeline. Andrea started to include her baby in her gardening time, spreading a blanket nearby or letting her little one play in the dirt. This small hobby became a precious routine, helping her feel more like herself and less overwhelmed by her new role as a mom.

Andrea's experience is a lot like Lydia's story. It reminds us that keeping our hobbies isn't just about having fun—it's about staying connected to who we are. Our interests can be a source of joy and renewal, making us better, more fulfilled moms.

Mom's Moments

Think about one hobby you loved before becoming a mom. This week, carve out a little time to do that activity. See how it makes you feel and think about how it can bring a positive change in your life. Maybe you can even involve your child, showing them the beauty of what you love.

Short Prayer

Dear God, help me find time for the hobbies that bring joy and peace to my life. Let me share this joy with my family and find refreshment in these moments. Amen.

29

SETTING REALISTIC PERSONAL GOALS

___ / ___ / _____

"Now Deborah, a prophet, the wife of Lappidoth, was leading Israel at that time. She held court under the Palm of Deborah between Ramah and Bethel in the hill country of Ephraim, and the Israelites went up to her to have their disputes decided."

— JUDGES 4:4-5

Balancing a million things at once, trying to keep your family happy while holding onto your own dreams, is a common struggle. Many of us face this challenge. As moms, it's easy to put our own goals on hold, but there is a way to balance both.

Deborah, a prophetess and judge, managed to balance her big responsibilities with her personal life. She led Israel and settled disputes, all while being a wife. Her story shows us that we can manage our duties at home and still pursue our dreams.

When I had my first baby, I was drowning in diapers, feedings, and sleepless nights. I felt like I had no time for myself. I remember sitting there one night, utterly exhausted, thinking, *"Will I ever have time for my own goals again?"*

That night, after putting my baby to sleep, I prayed for help. In that quiet moment, I felt a gentle nudge in my heart saying, *"Start small."* I decided to carve out just 15 minutes each day for myself. Sometimes I read a book, other times I journaled, and occasionally I just sat in silence, seeking God's peace.

These small moments added up. I started to feel more like myself, more patient, and better able to handle the daily chaos. The key was setting small, realistic goals and giving myself grace. Just like Deborah, who led her people with strength and wisdom, we can find a way to balance our roles by leaning on God's guidance.

Think about Deborah's journey. She didn't become a leader overnight. She was consistent and faithful in her duties. We can do the same by taking small steps toward our goals. Whether it's learning a new hobby, starting a small project, or taking care of our health, every little bit helps.

It's easy to get discouraged when we look at all we have to do and how far we want to go. But God doesn't expect us to do everything at once. He walks with us, giving us strength and wisdom each day. By setting realistic goals and seeking His guidance, we can balance our personal dreams with our family responsibilities.

Mom's Moments

Create a "Mom's Goal Board." Find a small board or even a piece of paper and write down your personal goals. Break them into tiny, achievable steps. Place it somewhere you'll see it every day. Celebrate each small victory with a smile or a treat, and remember to pray for strength and guidance as you move forward.

Short Prayer

Dear God, help me set realistic goals and balance my family responsibilities with my personal dreams. Guide me each step of the way. Amen.

30

STAYING IN TOUCH WITH FRIENDS WITHOUT KIDS

___ / ___ / _____

"At that time Mary got ready and hurried to a town in the hill country of Judea, where she entered Zechariah's home and greeted Elizabeth."

— LUKE 1:39-40

Have you ever found yourself reminiscing about those carefree days when you could spontaneously meet up with a friend for coffee or lunch? Now, as a new mom, even the simplest outings can feel like a Herculean task. There's the packing of the diaper bag, the timing of naps and feedings, and the endless unpredictability of a baby's mood. It's easy to feel like your social life has taken a backseat.

When Mary was young and newly pregnant with Jesus. She could have easily stayed home, overwhelmed by the incredible news she had received. Yet, instead of isolating herself, she chose to visit her cousin Elizabeth, who was also expecting a child. Despite their different stages in life, Mary knew the importance of maintaining their bond. She didn't let her new circumstances keep her from seeking companionship and support.

In the same way, your friendships don't have to drift apart because your life has taken a new direction. Your faith can be the guiding light that helps you nurture these relationships. It encourages you to look beyond the daily challenges and cherish the people who have always been there for you.

Consider your closest friend who doesn't have kids. Maybe she feels hesitant to reach out, unsure of how to fit into your new life. Or perhaps she misses the spontaneity of your pre-baby days and doesn't know how to reconnect. It's easy to let misunderstandings or assumptions create distance, but your faith can help bridge that gap. A quick text to share a funny moment, a short call to catch up, or a heartfelt message on social media can remind her that your friendship is still a priority.

I recall when my friend Grace, who doesn't have children, invited me out for a movie night. I was knee-deep in midnight feedings and diaper changes, and the thought of going out seemed daunting. But I decided to go. We didn't spend much time talking about my baby; instead, we laughed about old times, shared our current dreams, and reconnected on a deeper level. That evening reminded me that while my role as a mom is crucial, so is keeping my friendships alive. It's about finding a balance and showing my friends that they still matter.

Mom's Moments

Plan a fun outing that includes your friend without kids. Maybe it's a picnic at the park where your baby can play, or a brunch at a cozy café. Show her that your friendship still matters, and enjoy some quality time together, blending both your worlds.

Short Prayer

Dear God, help me balance motherhood and friendship, and show Your love through my actions. Amen.

_____

_____

_____

31

KEEPING FRIENDSHIPS STRONG

___ / ___ / _____

"But Ruth replied, 'Don't urge me to leave you or to turn back from you. Where you go I will go, and where you stay I will stay. Your people will be my people and your God my God. Where you die I will die, and there I will be buried. May the Lord deal with me, be it ever so severely, if even death separates you and me.'"

— RUTH 1:16-17

Have you ever felt like you're losing touch with friends because of motherhood? It's a beautiful but busy time, and keeping up with friends can be hard. Let's learn from Naomi and Ruth in the Bible about the power of loyal friendships.

When Naomi decided to go back to Bethlehem after losing her husband and sons, Ruth, her daughter-in-law, chose to stay with her. Ruth's promise, *"Where you go, I will go...,"* shows how strong their bond was. It wasn't just convenience; it was deep commitment.

As new moms, we often feel overwhelmed. With little sleep, endless diaper changes, and constant feedings, it can feel like there's no time for friends.

But just as Ruth's commitment to Naomi provided hope and strength, our friendships can do the same for us.

Angelica, a new mom who felt isolated. She missed spontaneous coffee dates and long chats with her best friend, Eden. Determined not to lose this connection, Krizza and Eden set up weekly video calls during the baby's nap time. These calls became a lifeline for Jessica, a place to share her struggles and joys without judgment. Their bond grew stronger because they made an effort to stay connected.

Or think about Megan, who started a *"Mom's Book Club"* with her friends. They chose short, inspiring reads and met once a month, bringing their babies along. This not only helped Megan keep her friendships but also created a support group where they shared parenting tips and encouraged each other.

Motherhood brings new challenges that can either weaken or strengthen our friendships. It's in these moments of need that we can truly appreciate the friends who stand by us. The story of Ruth and Naomi shows us that loyal friendships can be a great source of support and joy. They remind us that we don't have to go through this journey alone.

Mom's Moments

Plan a "friendship date" with a close friend. It could be a coffee meet-up, a walk in the park with your babies, or even a virtual catch-up if meeting in person is hard. Use this time to share your experiences, listen to each other, and pray together. Spending intentional time together can be really uplifting for both of you.

Short Prayer

Dear God, help me nurture my friendships with loyalty and love, just as Ruth did with Naomi. Give me the strength and wisdom to support my friends even in busy times. Amen.

32

CONNECTING WITH OTHER PARENTS

___ / ___ / _____

"Mary stayed with Elizabeth for about three months and then returned home."

— LUKE 1:56

Feeling alone in your journey as a new mother is common. The sleepless nights, the endless diaper changes, and the constant worry about whether you're doing everything right can feel overwhelming. Even Mary, the mother of Jesus, needed support. She found it in her cousin Elizabeth. Imagine the strength and comfort they found in each other, two mothers bound by their extraordinary circumstances, sharing their fears, joys, and faith.

Mary's visit to Elizabeth wasn't just a family reunion; it was a divine appointment. Mary, pregnant with Jesus, found solace in Elizabeth, who was carrying John the Baptist. Their bond was strengthened by shared experiences and mutual encouragement. This story highlights the importance of connecting with others who understand what you're going through.

Think about the first time you walked into a room full of other parents, perhaps at a playgroup or a church gathering. Did you feel nervous, unsure if anyone would understand what you were going through? Maybe you wondered if you would fit in or if you'd have anything in common with these other parents. This feeling is incredibly common. Just like you, Mary must have had her own uncertainties as she traveled to Elizabeth's home.

But the moment they greeted each other, any doubts faded. Elizabeth's baby leaped in her womb, and she was filled with the Holy Spirit, recognizing Mary's blessed condition. They shared three precious months together, filled with mutual encouragement, faith, and understanding. It was a time of preparation for both of them, made easier by the companionship they found in one another.

As a new mom, building relationships with other parents can provide you with a network of support. These connections can be found in various places—church groups, playdates, online forums, or community centers. Your faith plays a significant role in these relationships. It offers a foundation of shared values and a source of strength and encouragement. Just as Mary and Elizabeth uplifted each other, you can find and offer support through the bonds of faith.

Like Denise, a new mother who recently moved to a new city. She felt isolated and overwhelmed until she joined a moms' group at her local church. There, she met other mothers who were experiencing similar challenges. They shared tips, offered babysitting swaps, and most importantly, prayed for each other. These relationships transformed Denise's experience of motherhood from one of isolation to one of community.

In another instance, Jenny, a stay-at-home mom, started an online group for mothers in her area. Through virtual meetings and discussions, she connected with other moms, shared her faith, and found practical advice on parenting. These connections became a lifeline during tough times, proving that support can come in many forms.

Imagine joining a small group at your church, where you can share your journey and hear about others'. Or attending a community event where you meet another mom who becomes a close friend. These connections can make all the difference, providing you with practical advice, emotional support, and a reminder that you are not alone in this journey.

Mom's Moments

This week, make a deliberate effort to connect with another parent. It could be joining a local moms' group, arranging a playdate, or simply reaching out to another mom you've met. Share a scripture or a word of encouragement. Notice how these connections bless both of you, and think about ways you can continue to build and nurture these relationships.

Short Prayer

Dear God, Help me to connect with other parents and build supportive, faith-based relationships. Thank you for the blessing of community. Guide me to offer and receive encouragement. Amen.

33

SETTING BOUNDARIES WITH FAMILY

___ / ___ / _____

> *"But Hannah did not go up, for she said to her husband, 'Not until the child is weaned; then I will take him, that he may appear before the Lord and remain there forever.' So Elkanah her husband said to her, 'Do what seems best to you; wait until you have weaned him. Only let the Lord establish His word.' So the woman stayed and nursed her son until she had weaned him."*
>
> — 1 SAMUEL 1:22-23 (NKJV)

Have you ever felt the pressure of trying to balance family expectations with what you know is best for your child? Setting and keeping boundaries with family members can be one of the toughest parts of being a mom. I remember clearly the days after my first child was born. The joy and excitement were mixed with a flood of advice and opinions from well-meaning family members. Everyone had their own ideas about how I should raise my child, from feeding schedules to sleep routines. While I appreciated their wisdom and experience, I also felt a strong need to find my own way as a mother.

The story of Hannah speaks to me deeply. She made a promise to God that if He gave her a child, she would dedicate him to the Lord's service. When Samuel was born, Hannah stayed true to her promise by setting boundaries to make sure her vow was kept. Even when it meant going against what was normal or expected by her family, she stood firm in her decision. Her husband Elkanah supported her, knowing the importance of following God's plan.

Hannah's story shows us that setting boundaries out of love and faith is powerful. She waited until Samuel was weaned before bringing him to the Lord, even if others didn't understand. She put God's promise and her child's needs first. Setting boundaries wasn't about shutting others out; it was about making sure God's plan for Samuel was fulfilled.

Thinking about Hannah's story, I realized that setting boundaries is not just about saying no; it's about making a space where your family can grow according to God's plan. It means having the courage to trust the wisdom God has given you as a mother, even when others might not understand. When my mom insisted on certain traditions for my baby that didn't feel right to me, I kindly but firmly explained my reasons and stood my ground. It wasn't easy, but it brought peace and understanding to our family.

One example that stands out is when I decided to follow a specific feeding schedule that was different from what my mom did with me and my siblings. She was initially hurt and confused by my choice. However, I gently explained that I had prayed about it and felt led to this approach for my child's health and our family's routine. Over time, she saw the benefits and respected my decision. This experience taught me that while setting boundaries can be hard, it is important for creating a healthy and godly family life.

Mom's Moments

Take a few minutes to create a "Boundaries Plan." Write down one area where you need to set a boundary with family members. Explain why this boundary is important for you and your child, and think of kind but firm ways to communicate it. Pray for wisdom and clarity as you get ready to talk to your family. To practice, role-play the conversation with a friend or your spouse to build confidence.

Short Prayer

BIBLICAL TEACHINGS

Dear God, grant me the wisdom and courage to set boundaries that honor You and protect my family's well-being. Help me to communicate with love and grace. Amen.

34

GIVING ATTENTION TO ALL YOUR KIDS

___ / ___ / _____

> *"Now Israel loved Joseph more than any of his other sons, because he had been born to him in his old age; and he made an ornate robe for him. When his brothers saw that their father loved him more than any of them, they hated him and could not speak a kind word to him."*
>
> — GENESIS 37:3-4

Motherhood often feels like being pulled in a million different directions. Between work, household chores, and the constant demands of caring for children, it's easy to feel overwhelmed. Ensuring that each of your children feels loved and attended to when you're stretched thin is challenging. The story of Jacob and his sons offers valuable insights into the dynamics of parental love and favoritism.

Jacob, also known as Israel, had twelve sons. Out of all of them, he favored Joseph, the son born to him in his old age, and even made him a special, ornate robe. This act of favoritism led to jealousy and bitterness among his other sons, who felt neglected and unloved. Their resentment eventually led to a series of tragic events, illustrating the destructive power of perceived favoritism.

BIBLICAL TEACHINGS

Consider the story of Susan, a mother of three, who faced a similar challenge. Her eldest, Rachelle, was independent and often quiet. Her middle child, Joey, craved attention and was always seeking her approval. Her youngest, Olivia, was still a baby and demanded constant care. Susan often found herself stretched thin, trying to meet the unique needs of each child while managing her household and a demanding job.

One evening, after a particularly chaotic day, Susan sat down with a cup of tea, feeling utterly exhausted. She remembered the story of Jacob and Joseph, and it struck a chord with her. She realized that in her efforts to juggle everything, she might be unintentionally neglecting the emotional needs of her children. Determined to make a change, Sarah decided to set aside individual time for each child, no matter how brief.

With Rachelle, she began having heart-to-heart talks about her day at school, her friends, and her dreams. This helped Rachelle feel more connected and valued. With Joey, she dedicated time to play his favorite games and engage in activities that made him feel special and appreciated. For baby Olivia, Sarah made sure to enjoy quiet moments of cuddling and singing lullabies, creating a sense of security and love.

This intentional effort to connect with each child transformed the dynamics in Susan's home. Rachelle started opening up more, feeling more secure in her mother's love. Joey's need for constant validation decreased as he felt more assured of his place in the family. Even little Olivia seemed more content, sensing the loving atmosphere around her. The change wasn't immediate or without challenges, but the overall atmosphere in the home became more harmonious.

Susan's also found that leaning on God's wisdom and strength in her prayers provided her with the patience and discernment needed to nurture each child uniquely. She realized that God's grace was sufficient for her weaknesses and that His love was the ultimate model for her own.

In our busy lives, it's easy to overlook the individual needs of our children. We might think we are giving enough by providing for them physically, but emotional and spiritual nurturing is equally important. Just as God knows and loves each of us individually, He calls us to do the same with our children. By dedicating specific time and attention to each child, we can help them grow into confident, loving individuals who feel secure in their family's love and support.

Mom's Moments

This week, create a "date" with each of your children. It doesn't have to be elaborate—a simple walk in the park, a special story time, or even cooking a meal together. Let each child choose an activity they love. This special time will help reinforce their sense of being loved and valued individually.

Short Prayer

Dear God, grant me the wisdom to love and nurture each of my children uniquely, ensuring they all feel your love through me. Guide me to balance my time and energy so that each of my children feels special and valued. Amen.

MOM POWER: REFLECT & RENEW

DATE

S M T W T F S

REFLECTION

Sharing Parenting Duties

Reflect on how you and your partner share parenting responsibilities. What are each of your strengths, and how can you support each other better?

_____
_____
_____

Maintaining Connection

Think about a time when parenting made you feel distant from your partner. How did you handle it, and what can you do now to improve your relationship?

_____
_____
_____

PLANNING AHEAD

Supporting Different Parenting Styles

Pick one way you and your partner parent differently. How can you both support each other's styles to create a better environment for your child?

AREA OF DIFFERENCE:

PLAN FOR SUPPORT:

CREATIVE ACTIVITY

Create a Connection Jar

Write down simple activities you can do with your partner to reconnect, such as a quiet walk, a shared prayer time, or a special dessert. Pull one out each week to keep your relationship strong.

BIBLE VERSE REFLECTION

Acts 18:26
Priscilla and Aquila invited him to their home and explained to him the way of God more adequately.

Your Reflection

_____

_____

_____

Practical Aspects of
PARENTING

35

CHANGING DIAPERS QUICKLY

___ / ___ / _____

"And she gave birth to her firstborn, a son. She wrapped him in cloths and placed him in a manger, because there was no guest room available for them."

— LUKE 2:7

Have you ever found yourself in the middle of changing a diaper, only to face an unexpected mess or a wiggly baby? It's one of those everyday tasks that can feel never-ending, especially when you're tired and dealing with the constant demands of motherhood. Yet, even in these moments, there is an opportunity to find grace and connection.

Picture Mary, the mother of Jesus, wrapping her newborn in cloths and placing Him in a manger. Imagine the humility and love in that scene. Mary was in a stable, far from the comfort of home, yet she cared for Jesus with such tenderness. Her example shows us that grace can be found in the most ordinary tasks, even in changing diapers.

As a mom, I've been there many times. I remember one particularly hectic morning when my little one had a diaper blowout just as we were about to leave for an appointment. I was exhausted, running on just a few hours of sleep, and felt my patience wearing thin. But then I took a deep breath and remembered Mary's grace. Instead of rushing and getting frustrated, I slowed down and turned the moment into a bonding experience. I talked softly to my baby, made silly faces, and turned a messy situation into a moment of connection.

Making diaper changing quick and efficient can be much easier with a few practical tips, inspired by the grace and patience Mary exemplified.

First, preparation is key. Keep a diaper-changing station stocked with wipes, fresh diapers, diaper cream, and a change of clothes within reach. This minimizes interruptions and keeps you focused.

Developing a routine can also make a big difference. Babies thrive on routine, so establishing a consistent diaper-changing routine helps your baby know what to expect, reducing fussiness and making the process smoother.

Engaging and distracting your baby can be very helpful. Keep a small toy or a favorite book nearby to entertain them during diaper changes. Singing a song or talking to them can also keep them calm and cooperative.

Finally, practice makes perfect. The more you practice, the quicker and more efficient you will become. Don't be discouraged by initial struggles—every mom goes through them. Remember, each diaper change is an opportunity to connect with your baby.

Mom's Moments

Next time you're changing a diaper, try making it a special moment. Sing a silly song, tell a little story, or make funny faces to see your baby smile. Not only will this make the task more enjoyable, but it also helps you bond with your little one.

Short Prayer

Dear God, help me find grace in everyday tasks and to see the beauty in caring for my baby, just as Mary cared for Jesus. Amen.

36

BABYPROOFING YOUR HOME

___ / ___ / _____

> *"The wise woman builds her house, but with her own hands the foolish one tears hers down."*
>
> — PROVERBS 14:1

Have you ever wondered how to create a safe and nurturing environment for your baby that mirrors God's protective love? When I had my first child, I quickly realized that babyproofing wasn't just about keeping my little one safe; it was also about creating a home that reflects God's care and wisdom.

I remember one particular Saturday afternoon vividly. My son, barely crawling, had managed to find his way into every nook and cranny of our living room. It was then I realized that babyproofing wasn't just a task on a checklist; it was a continual act of love and vigilance. I started with the basics: covering electrical outlets, securing heavy furniture, and installing baby gates. But it wasn't until I saw my little one reach for a cabinet filled with cleaning supplies that the full weight of my responsibility hit me.

In that moment, I recalled Proverbs 14:1, which speaks of a wise woman building her house. Babyproofing became more than just a physical task; it was a spiritual endeavor, reflecting the care and foresight God has for us. By taking these steps, I was not only protecting my child but also instilling a sense of security and love that mirrored God's own protection over us.

One particular incident stands out in my memory. I had just finished installing a baby gate at the top of the stairs when my daughter, who was just starting to toddle, made a beeline for it. As I watched her shake the gate with her tiny hands, I felt a wave of gratitude. That gate was not just a barrier; it was a symbol of the care and effort I put into safeguarding her well-being. It reminded me of the many unseen ways God places "gates" in our lives to protect us from harm.

As my children grew, so did the complexity of babyproofing. I learned to anticipate their curiosity and adventurous spirits. I found creative hacks: using pool noodles to cover sharp edges of furniture, placing bells on doors to know when they are opened, and securing drawers with simple, inexpensive latches. Each hack not only kept my baby safe but also gave me peace of mind, knowing that I was taking active steps to build a safe haven for my family.

Babyproofing also taught me valuable lessons about trust and vigilance. It wasn't enough to simply install safety measures; I had to remain attentive and proactive, much like our relationship with God. We must continually seek His guidance and wisdom, ensuring our spiritual *"house"* is built on a firm foundation. Just as we babyproof our homes, we must also guard our hearts and minds, trusting in God's protection and provision.

Mom's Moments

Choose one room and make it your "safe haven" project. Identify hazards, babyproof thoroughly, and pray as you work, reflecting on God's protection. Share your tips with other moms in your community or online.

Short Prayer

Dear God, grant me wisdom and diligence as I create a safe environment for my baby. Help me reflect Your love and care in my home. Amen.

37

PICKING BABY GEAR ON A BUDGET

___ / ___ / _____

"She considers a field and buys it; out of her earnings she plants a vineyard."

— PROVERBS 31:16

Standing in the baby gear aisle, overwhelmed by the endless options and hefty price tags, is a common experience. It's easy to get caught up in the latest trends and gadgets, believing that our babies need the most expensive items to thrive. However, wisdom and discernment, not the highest price tag, guide the best choices.

The Proverbs 31 woman exemplifies this wisdom, managing her household with care and meeting her family's needs without extravagance. When I was expecting my first child, I felt the pressure to buy everything—from the top-of-the-line stroller to fancy nursery decor. But I knew our budget couldn't stretch that far.

I turned to God for guidance, praying for wisdom like the Proverbs 31 woman. Through prayer and thoughtful research, I discovered that many high-priced items had affordable, equally effective alternatives. I learned to distinguish between wants and needs, focusing on essentials like a safe car seat, a sturdy crib, and comfortable clothing.

One of the most memorable experiences was setting up the nursery. I had envisioned a beautifully decorated room with matching furniture and stylish decor. However, the reality of our budget meant I had to get creative. I found a second-hand crib that was in excellent condition, and with a little bit of paint and some new bedding, it looked perfect. I also discovered that hand-me-downs from friends and family were a great way to save money without compromising on quality.

I realized that many of the so-called *"essential"* baby items were more about convenience than necessity. For example, a simple changing pad placed on a dresser worked just as well as an expensive changing table. A basic baby monitor provided the peace of mind I needed without all the extra features of the high-end models.

As I made these decisions, I felt a sense of peace knowing that God was guiding me. Each choice became an act of trust, believing that God would provide what we needed. And He did. From unexpected gifts to timely sales, our needs were met in ways that reaffirmed my faith.

In those early months, I also found that the most important things I could provide for my baby were love, attention, and a sense of security. These didn't come from expensive gadgets but from my presence and care. The Proverbs 31 woman reminds us that wise stewardship and love are the cornerstones of a well-managed household.

Mom's Moments

Create a list of baby gear essentials and set a budget. Organize a "baby gear swap" with other moms in your community or church. Bring gently used items to trade, fostering a supportive network and saving money.

Short Prayer

Dear God, grant me wisdom to make wise choices for my baby without straining our finances. Help me to trust in Your provision and prioritize what truly matters. Thank you for Your constant guidance and love. Amen.

38

DEALING WITH COMMON BABY ILLNESSES

___ / ___ / _____

"When the child had grown, he went out one day to his father among the reapers. And he said to his father, 'Oh, my head, my head!' The father said to his servant, 'Carry him to his mother.' And when he had lifted him and brought him to his mother, the child sat on her lap till noon, and then he died. And she went up and laid him on the bed of the man of God and shut the door behind him and went out."

— 2 KINGS 4:18-21

Every new mother has found herself in the throes of worry, cradling her precious baby in her arms, uncertain whether to wait it out or rush to the doctor. The story of the Shunammite woman from the Bible offers a profound lesson in faith and action.

One hot day, the Shunammite woman's son complained of a severe headache while out in the fields with his father. Her husband instructed a servant to carry the boy to his mother, and she instinctively took him in her arms, comforting him. Despite her best efforts, the boy's condition worsened, and he eventually stopped breathing.

In a moment of sheer crisis, she didn't succumb to despair. Instead, she took a bold step of faith. She laid her son on the bed of the prophet Elisha, closed the door, and set out to find the man of God. Her actions were a testament to her belief in God's power and her deep-rooted faith. She knew where to seek help, balancing her natural motherly instincts with divine intervention.

As a mother, you may face similar moments of uncertainty when your baby falls ill. It's important to trust your instincts and seek medical help when needed. At the same time, prayer can bring peace and guidance.

When my own children were young, I remember countless nights spent by their bedside, listening to their labored breathing or feeling their feverish brows. One particular night stands out in my memory. My youngest had a persistent cough that seemed to worsen as the night wore on. I sat there, heart racing, debating whether to wait until morning or rush to the emergency room.

I whispered a desperate prayer, asking God for guidance. In that stillness, I felt a sense of calm wash over me. I remembered the story of the Shunammite woman and her unwavering faith. I decided to call our pediatrician, who reassured me and gave clear instructions on how to care for my child through the night. My baby recovered, and I was reminded of the importance of balancing faith with practical action.

Mom's Moments

Create a "Health Journal" for your baby. Document symptoms, your actions, medical advice, and outcomes. Reflect in prayer, thanking God for His guidance and asking for wisdom. This will serve as both a reference and a reminder of God's faithfulness through each challenge.

Short Prayer

Dear God, grant me wisdom and calmness in caring for my baby. Help me to know when to seek help and to trust in Your healing power. Keep my baby safe and healthy. Amen.

39

BUDGETING FOR BABY EXPENSES

___ / ___ / _____

"The jar of oil did not run dry, in keeping with the word of the LORD spoken by Elijah."

— 2 KINGS 4:1-7

Have you ever stood in the baby aisle of a store, feeling completely overwhelmed by the number of things your baby needs? I certainly have. When my first baby was born, the expenses seemed endless—diapers, clothes, formula, baby gear, and so much more. It felt like every time I turned around, there was another cost I hadn't anticipated.

One evening, I found myself worrying about how we would manage all these new expenses. That's when I turned to the Bible and found comfort in the story of the widow and her oil in 2 Kings 4:1-7. This story resonated deeply with me. The widow was in a desperate situation, just like I felt at times. She had only a small jar of oil, but through her faith and obedience, God multiplied her resources beyond what she could have imagined.

I remember sitting down with my husband, both of us feeling the weight of financial stress. We prayed for wisdom and guidance, asking God to help us manage our money wisely. Together, we created a budget, starting with our essential expenses and then figuring out how to fit in all the baby needs. We had to make some tough decisions and sacrifices, but we trusted that God would provide for us.

In those early months, we saw God's provision in many unexpected ways. Friends and family surprised us with gifts of gently used baby clothes and gear. We discovered sales and coupons that made a big difference in our budget. One day, when our supply of diapers was running low, a neighbor knocked on our door with a big box of diapers her baby had outgrown. It felt like a little miracle, reminding us that God was looking out for us.

There were still times when our faith wavered, and we wondered how we would make ends meet. But every time we turned to God in prayer, He provided what we needed. Just like the widow's oil, our resources didn't run dry. We learned that budgeting wasn't just about numbers; it was about trusting in God's provision and being good stewards of what He had given us.

One particularly tough month, our budget was tighter than ever. Our baby needed more formula, and we weren't sure how we'd afford it. We prayed for help and trusted that God would provide. The next day, I found a surprise package on our doorstep from a friend who knew our situation. Inside were several cans of formula and some baby food. I was overwhelmed with gratitude and relief, knowing that God had answered our prayers through the kindness of others.

Mom's Moments

Write a list of ways to save on baby expenses—swap clothes with a friend, look for sales, or make homemade baby food. Share one tip with a fellow mom. Trust that God will guide and provide as you seek to be a wise steward.

Short Prayer

Dear God, help me trust in Your provision and be wise in managing our resources. Thank You for always providing for my baby and our family. Amen.

40

SAVING MONEY ON BABY ESSENTIALS

___ / ___ / _____

"She sees that her trading is profitable, and her lamp does not go out at night."

— PROVERBS 31:18

Have you ever looked at your baby budget and felt overwhelmed? The cost of diapers, clothes, toys, and other essentials can add up quickly. The Proverbs 31 woman teaches us that with wisdom and careful planning, we can manage our resources well and still provide the best for our families.

When I had my first baby, I was caught off guard by how quickly expenses piled up. I wanted my child to have everything they needed, but I also had to be mindful of our family budget. It was a challenging balance to strike. During this time, I often turned to Proverbs 31 for guidance and reassurance.

One of the first things I did was to rethink our needs versus wants. I joined a local mom group and discovered the incredible value of second-hand baby items. Many moms were eager to pass on clothes, toys, and even furniture that their children had outgrown. These items were often in great condition and cost a fraction of the price of new ones. This not only saved us money but also introduced me to a supportive community of other moms.

I also found that making some baby essentials at home could save money and be fun. For example, instead of buying expensive baby wipes, I made my own using soft cloths and a gentle homemade solution. It was simple, cost-effective, and better for my baby's skin.

Couponing became another valuable skill. I started collecting coupons from newspapers, online sources, and even directly from stores. I would plan our shopping trips around sales and discounts. It was amazing how much we could save with a little effort and planning. Every time I saved money, I felt a deep sense of gratitude and thanked God for the resources and wisdom He provided.

Another tip that helped was creating a baby registry with only the essentials. By focusing on what we truly needed, we avoided the temptation to buy unnecessary items. Friends and family were more than happy to help with the items on our list, which eased the financial burden even more.

Mom's Moments

This week, try visiting a local mom group or online marketplace to find gently used baby items. Challenge yourself to create one homemade baby essential, like wipes or baby food. Reflect on how these small changes can add up to significant savings and bring a sense of community into your life.

Short Prayer

Dear God, thank You for providing for our needs and giving us the wisdom to manage our resources. Help me to make wise and frugal choices for my family. Amen.

_____

_____

_____

_____

41

PLANNING FOR FUTURE EXPENSES LIKE EDUCATION

___ / ___ / _____

"And she made a vow, saying, 'Lord Almighty, if you will only look on your servant's misery and remember me, and not forget your servant but give her a son, then I will give him to the Lord for all the days of his life, and no razor will ever be used on his head.'"

— 1 SAMUEL 1:11

Have you ever found yourself lying awake at night, worrying about how you will afford your child's education? As parents, we all want to give our children the best opportunities in life, and education is a significant part of that dream. But the thought of paying for it can be overwhelming. How can we plan wisely and trust God in the process?

Consider the story of Hannah in the Bible. She longed for a child and made a heartfelt promise to God. She vowed that if He blessed her with a son, she would dedicate him to the Lord's service for his entire life. God heard her prayers, and Samuel was born. Hannah's dedication was not just about Samuel's immediate upbringing but also about his future and his purpose.

Hannah's faith and dedication offer a powerful lesson for us. While we might not be making the same vows, we can learn from her trust in God's plan for her son. Planning for our children's future, especially their education, involves both practical steps and a deep reliance on God's guidance.

Let's bring this closer to home. I remember a time when I was juggling bills and barely making ends meet. The idea of setting aside money for my child's college fund seemed impossible. I felt a pang of guilt every time I thought about it. But then I remembered Hannah's story and decided to take a small step of faith. I started setting aside a small amount each month, no matter how tight things were. It wasn't much, but it was a start.

One mother I know started a college fund for her daughter when she was just a baby. Each month, she set aside a small amount, trusting that God would provide. Despite unexpected expenses and financial strains, she remained committed. By the time her daughter graduated high school, there was enough to cover her first year of college. This mother's story illustrates that while our efforts are essential, God's provision and timing are perfect.

Sometimes, it's easy to feel like our small contributions won't make a difference. But God sees our efforts and multiplies them. Just like the loaves and fishes, He can turn our small savings into a substantial provision for our children's future.

Mom's Moments

Write down one practical step you can take this month to start saving for your child's education. Then, set a small, achievable savings goal for this month, even if it's just a few dollars. Lastly, find a verse or prayer to say each time you add to the savings, reminding yourself of God's provision.

Short Prayer

Dear God, grant me wisdom and peace as I plan for my child's future. Help me trust in Your provision. Amen.

42

BALANCING FINANCIAL PRIORITIES WITH FAMILY NEEDS

___ / ___ / _____

> *"She is not afraid of snow for her household, for all her household are clothed in scarlet."*
>
> — PROVERBS 31:21 (ESV)

Have you ever stayed up at night, worrying about how to pay all the bills and still meet your family's needs? Balancing money and family needs can be very stressful. I remember a month when everything seemed to go wrong at once—our car broke down, the kids needed new shoes, and we had unexpected medical bills. It felt like too much to handle.

During that tough time, I found comfort in the story of the virtuous woman from Proverbs 31. This woman faced many challenges, yet she managed her household with grace and wisdom. She wasn't worried about the cold winter because she had prepared ahead. Her family had warm clothes because of her hard work and careful planning. It wasn't just about being good at managing money; it was about having faith in God's help and wisdom.

Today, managing money can feel like trying to keep too many balls in the air. There are always bills to pay, groceries to buy, and unexpected expenses. It's easy to feel overwhelmed. But just like the virtuous woman, we can handle these challenges with faith.

Start by taking a deep breath and asking God for guidance. Then, look at your finances with fresh eyes. Are there areas where you can cut back? Maybe there are small changes you can make that will add up over time. Trusting God doesn't mean we don't have to work hard or make tough decisions, but it does mean we're not alone in our efforts.

Think about the virtuous woman. She worked hard, yes, but she also trusted that God would provide for her family. We can do the same. It's not about being perfect; it's about making progress and relying on God's wisdom.

Mom's Moments

Sit down with your spouse or a trusted friend and talk about your money goals and challenges. Make a simple budget together that covers your family's needs and shows your trust in God's help. Also, try to save a small amount each week for emergencies—this can help reduce future stress and show your faith in God's provision.

Short Prayer

Dear God, help me balance our money wisely and trust in Your help. Guide me as I provide for my family's needs with faith and wisdom. Amen.

43

CHOOSING CHILDCARE THAT FITS YOUR VALUES

___ / ___ / _____

> *"Pharaoh's daughter said to her, 'Take this baby and nurse him for me, and I will pay you.' So the woman took the baby and nursed him."*
>
> — EXODUS 2:9

Choosing childcare involves numerous factors and often requires deep prayer for discernment. The story of Jochebed, Moses' mother, serves as a powerful reminder of the importance of trust and faith in our children's care. Faced with an impossible situation, Jochebed placed Moses in a basket and entrusted him to the waters of the Nile, ultimately placing him in the hands of Pharaoh's daughter.

Like Jochebed experienced, choosing childcare means trusting that God will guide us to the right environment for our child. When my eldest was born, I visited many childcare centers, each offering different programs and values. I had non-negotiables: loving caregivers, a nurturing environment, and a place where Christian values were upheld. Every night, I prayed for wisdom, and God led us to the right place—a center where we felt peace, and our values were embraced.

I vividly recall one visit where the center had all the latest gadgets and educational toys, but something felt off. Another had a warm, home-like atmosphere, but the caregivers seemed overwhelmed and distant. Finally, we found a small center run by a lovely woman who treated every child as her own. There was a sense of calm and genuine care. During my visit, I noticed how she took time with each child, not rushing through tasks but giving them her full attention. This reminded me of how Jochebed must have felt, entrusting her precious child to someone who would care deeply for him.

The decision process was not easy. There were moments of doubt and anxiety. However, in those times, I remembered Jochebed's faith and leaned into prayer even more. I asked God to make it clear which path to take, and to give me peace about the decision. And He did. The right choice was illuminated not by flashy brochures or modern amenities, but by the sense of God's presence and peace.

Jochebed had to trust God with her baby's very life. Today, we might not face the same dangers, but the emotional weight can feel just as heavy. Trusting someone else with your child is never easy. It requires prayer, discernment, and sometimes, stepping out in faith.

Mom's Moments

Create a "Childcare Choice" journal. List your non-negotiables, prayers, and reflections during your search. Reflect on Jochebed's trust in God with Moses and pray daily for guidance. Share your journey with a fellow mom and support each other in prayer.

Short Prayer

Dear God, grant me wisdom and discernment as I seek the best childcare for my baby. Help me trust in Your guidance and find peace in Your decision. Surround my child with Your love and protection always. Amen.

44

GETTING READY TO BE AWAY FROM BABY

___ / ___ / _____

> *"I prayed for this child, and the Lord has granted me what I asked of him. So now I give him to the Lord. For his whole life he will be given over to the Lord."*
>
> — 1 SAMUEL 1:27-28

Have you ever wondered how you would cope with leaving your precious baby in someone else's care? The thought alone can bring a wave of anxiety and doubt. When I faced this transition, I found myself wrestling with fear and guilt, unsure if anyone else could love and protect my child as I do.

Hannah's story of leaving Samuel at the temple always struck a chord with me. Imagine the emotional turmoil she must have experienced, entrusting her beloved son to Eli after years of fervent prayer and waiting. Yet, Hannah's faith in God's plan and her dedication to His will is profoundly inspiring. She knew that God had a purpose for Samuel that extended beyond her immediate presence.

I remember my first day back at work after my maternity leave. The night before, I held my baby close, my heart heavy with the thought of separation. But as I prayed, I felt a comforting assurance. God reminded me that just as He watched over Samuel, He would watch over my child. It wasn't easy, but each day, I leaned on His promises, finding strength in knowing that His care is perfect and His love unending.

The morning of my return to work, I felt a mix of emotions—sadness, anxiety, and even a little excitement about returning to a routine. I whispered a prayer over my sleeping baby, asking God to keep him safe and happy. Throughout the day, I found myself glancing at the clock, my thoughts drifting back home. But each time worry crept in, I reminded myself of Hannah's unwavering trust in God's plan. Just as she placed Samuel's future in God's hands, I knew I could trust God with my child's well-being.

The drive to work felt longer than usual, with every stoplight and turn pulling me farther away from my little one. I played a recording of his laughter on my phone to comfort myself, and as I listened, I remembered the countless ways God had shown His faithfulness in my life. If He had guided me through past challenges, surely He would guide me through this one too.

Throughout the day, I checked in with the caregiver, finding solace in pictures and updates. My heart warmed seeing my baby's smiles, knowing he was in good hands. Each time a pang of guilt or worry surfaced, I paused to pray, asking God for peace and reassurance. Slowly, I began to see this new phase not as a loss, but as an opportunity—for my baby to learn and grow, and for me to rely more deeply on God's grace and provision.

Mom's Moments

Plan a "Faith and Comfort" kit for your baby's caregiver. Include a favorite blanket, a small toy, a family photo, and a handwritten prayer. This kit not only provides comfort to your baby but also reassures you that you are sharing God's love and care even when you are apart.

Short Prayer

Dear God, Help me trust You with my baby's care as I step into this new chapter. Guide and protect us always. Amen.

45

ASKING FOR WHAT YOU NEED AT WORK

___ / ___ / _____

> *"Go, gather together all the Jews who are in Susa, and fast for me. Do not eat or drink for three days, night or day. I and my attendants will fast as you do. When this is done, I will go to the king, even though it is against the law. And if I perish, I perish."*
>
> — ESTHER 4:16

Have you ever found yourself hesitant to ask for what you need at work, fearing judgment or rejection? It's a common struggle, especially for new moms balancing the demands of a career and motherhood. I vividly remember the first time I needed to ask for a more flexible schedule after my first child was born. The anxiety was overwhelming. Would my request be seen as a lack of commitment? Would it affect my career growth?

In the Bible, Esther faced a much more daunting challenge. She had to advocate for her people, risking her life to approach the king without being summoned. Her courage and reliance on God are profoundly inspiring. Esther called on her community to fast and pray with her, drawing strength from her faith and the support of others. It was a pivotal moment where her bravery and trust in God's plan saved her people.

Similarly, when I needed accommodations at work, I leaned heavily on my faith. I prayed for wisdom and strength, and I sought counsel from trusted friends and family. I prepared my case thoughtfully, presenting how flexible hours would benefit both my family and my work productivity. To my relief, my request was granted, and it not only improved my work-life balance but also set a precedent for other new mothers in my workplace. It was a reminder that God's guidance can lead us to advocate not only for ourselves but also pave the way for others.

Esther's story teaches the value of courage, faith, and preparation. Whether you're asking for flexible hours, a quiet room for pumping, or other support, remember that God is with you. You are not alone in these challenges.

Mom's Moments

Reflect on a time you needed to ask for something at work. How did you feel? Create a "support circle" of trusted colleagues or friends who can offer advice and encouragement. Role-play the conversation with someone to build confidence. Also, consider mentoring other new moms in your workplace who may face similar challenges.

Short Prayer

Dear God, grant me the courage and wisdom to advocate for what I need at work, knowing You are with me every step of the way. Help me to be a support for others as well. Amen.

_____

_____

_____

_____

_____

46

CHANGING CAREER GOALS AFTER BECOMING A MOM

___ / ___ / _____

"And Ruth the Moabite said to Naomi, 'Let me go to the fields and pick up the leftover grain behind anyone in whose eyes I find favor.' Naomi said to her, 'Go ahead, my daughter.' So she went out, entered a field and began to glean behind the harvesters."

— RUTH 2:2-3

When you embrace the beautiful journey of motherhood, your career goals often shift in unexpected ways. Just like Ruth, who found herself in a new land with new responsibilities, many of us face unexpected changes in our career paths after becoming mothers. Ruth's story is a powerful reminder that God can use every season of our lives for His greater purpose.

Before becoming a mother, I had a clear career path mapped out. My goals were defined, and my steps were ordered. I was climbing the corporate ladder, hitting milestones, and chasing dreams that I believed were my calling. But when I held my first baby, everything changed. My priorities shifted, and my heart longed to be present for every milestone, every giggle, and every tear. Just like Ruth who stepped into the unknown to provide for her family, I found myself stepping into a new phase of life where my career ambitions had to be re-evaluated.

Ruth's faithfulness shows us it's okay for our goals to change. The important thing is seeking God's guidance in every step. As mothers, we may find that our careers need to adapt, and that's perfectly okay.

I remember wrestling with the decision to step back from a demanding job to be more present for my children. The guilt was overwhelming, but through prayer, God reassured me that this new role was just as valuable. He reminded me that the skills I gained in my career could be used in unexpected ways that align with my life as a mother.

Take time to reflect on how your career goals have shifted since becoming a mom. Seek God's will in this new season. Maybe you're called to stay home, start a new venture, or discover new passions. Whatever your path, know that God is with you, guiding your steps just as He did with Ruth.

Embracing career changes doesn't mean giving up on your dreams; it means trusting God's plans. Ruth's story shows us that following God's guidance leads to abundance, even if it looks different than we envisioned.

Mom's Moments

Create a vision board for your career and motherhood goals. Include images, quotes, and Bible verses that inspire you. Spend time each week praying over your board and asking God to guide your steps. This helps you visualize your goals and focus on what truly matters.

Short Prayer

Dear God, guide me in this new season of life as I balance motherhood and career. Help me to seek Your will in every decision I make. Bless my efforts and let them glorify You. Amen.

MOM POWER: REFLECT & RENEW

DATE

S M T W T F S

REFLECTION

Changing Diapers with Grace

Recall a time when a simple task with your baby felt special. How did it make you feel, and how can you keep finding joy in daily parenting?

_____
_____
_____

Babyproofing Your Home

Think about the steps you've taken or plan to take to babyproof your home. How does creating a safe environment reflect your care and love for your child?

_____
_____
_____

PLANNING AHEAD

Choosing Childcare That Fits Your Values

What are the key values and qualities you look for in a childcare provider? How can you ensure these align with your family's beliefs and needs?

KEY VALUES:	PLAN FOR CHOOSING:

CREATIVE ACTIVITY

Create a Faith and Comfort Kit

Prepare a small kit for your baby's caregiver that includes items like a favorite blanket, a comforting toy, a family photo, and a prayer. How can this kit help your baby feel secure and loved while you are away?

BIBLE VERSE REFLECTION

Exodus 2:9
Pharaoh's daughter said to her, 'Take this baby and nurse him for me, and I will pay you.' So the woman took the baby and nursed him.

Your Reflection

Family Dynamics &
FINDING JOY

47

AGREEING ON PARENTING STYLES

___ / ___ / _____

> *"When Joseph and Mary had done everything required by the Law of the Lord, they returned to Galilee to their own town of Nazareth. And the child grew and became strong; he was filled with wisdom, and the grace of God was on him."*
>
> — LUKE 2:39-40

I remember when my partner and I first started talking about how we wanted to raise our child. It seemed like there were so many decisions to make—everything from discipline to bedtime routines to what kind of values we wanted to instill. We both came from different backgrounds and had our own ideas about what parenting should look like, which made these conversations both exciting and a bit nerve-wracking.

There were times we didn't see eye to eye. I wanted to be more lenient, while my partner believed in firmer boundaries. It wasn't always easy to find common ground, and I'll admit, there were times when our discussions turned into debates. But through it all, we kept coming back to one thing: our shared faith.

Our faith became the anchor in our conversations about parenting. We realized that, above all else, we both wanted to raise our child in a way that reflected the values we hold dear—love, kindness, patience, and a deep sense of faith in God. We spent time praying together, asking God to guide us and help us make decisions that would honor Him and support our child's growth.

I often think about Mary and Joseph and how they must have navigated the challenges of raising Jesus together. They didn't have all the answers, but they trusted in God's plan and worked together to do what was best for their child. They were united in their mission to fulfill God's will, even when things weren't easy.

Looking back, I'm grateful for the times we've disagreed and worked through our differences. Those moments have made us stronger as a couple and more confident as parents. We're still learning, and I'm sure we'll continue to face new challenges as our child grows, but I know that as long as we keep our faith at the center, we'll be able to navigate whatever comes our way.

Mom's Moments

Think about a time when you and your partner had to make a parenting decision. How did your shared faith guide you? Reflect on how faith has helped you find common ground and strengthen your partnership as parents.

Short Prayer

Dear God, thank You for guiding us as we navigate the challenges of parenting. Help us to keep our faith at the center of our decisions and to support each other with love and patience. Amen.

_____

_____

_____

48

HANDLING GRANDPARENTS' & FAMILY EXCEPECTATIONS

___ / ___ / _____

> *"I will do whatever you say," Ruth answered. So she went down to the threshing floor and did everything her mother-in-law told her to do."*
>
> — RUTH 3:5-6

As a new parent, you're likely receiving advice from all directions—especially from grandparents and extended family. While their wisdom and experience can be invaluable, it can also feel overwhelming at times. Each person seems to have their own ideas about how you should raise your child, from what to feed them to how to handle bedtime routines. Navigating these expectations can be challenging, especially when they don't align with your own parenting style or beliefs.

It's important to remember that most advice, even when unsolicited, comes from a place of love and concern. Your family wants what's best for your child, just as you do. However, that doesn't mean you need to follow every piece of advice you're given. Balancing respect for your family's input with confidence in your own decisions is key.

Think about Ruth and Naomi. Ruth deeply respected her mother-in-law and often followed her guidance. However, Ruth also had to navigate her own path and make decisions that were right for her and her future. She honored Naomi's wisdom, but she also sought God's guidance in the choices she made. This balance of respect and discernment is something you can apply in your own life.

When faced with family expectations, start by listening with an open heart. Acknowledge the love and experience behind the advice, and thank them for their input. Then, take time to reflect and pray about what's been shared. Ask God for wisdom to discern which advice aligns with the values and parenting approach you and your partner have chosen. Remember, you are the one God has entrusted with this child, and He will guide you in making the best decisions for your family.

It's also okay to set boundaries when needed. If certain advice or expectations feel overwhelming or conflict with your approach, gently and respectfully communicate your decisions. Let your family know that while you value their input, you're making choices that you believe are best for your child. This isn't always easy, but it's important to stand firm in your role as a parent.

Mom's Moments

Reflect on a time when you had to navigate the expectations or advice of grandparents or extended family. How did you handle it? How did you seek God's wisdom in making your decision? Take a moment to pray for guidance in future situations.

Short Prayer

Dear God, thank You for the love and wisdom of our families. Help me to navigate their advice with grace and discernment. Give me the wisdom to make decisions that honor You and are best for my child. Amen.

_____

_____

49

CELEBRATING SMALL WINS

___ / ___ / _____

> *"Sarah said, 'God has brought me laughter, and everyone who hears about this will laugh with me.'"*
>
> — GENESIS 21:6

Have you ever felt overwhelmed by the enormity of motherhood? The endless cycle of feeding, changing, and soothing can often make us feel like we're merely surviving rather than thriving. But what if we shifted our focus and celebrated the small wins along the way?

One morning, after a sleepless night with my newborn, I found myself feeling utterly defeated. The baby was fussy, and I was running on fumes. As I sat on the couch, cradling my little one, I felt tears welling up. Then, out of nowhere, my baby gave me her first real smile. It was a fleeting moment, but it felt like a ray of sunshine piercing through a cloudy day. In that instant, I felt God's presence so profoundly, reminding me that joy can be found even in the smallest of victories.

Sarah, in the Bible, experienced a monumental win with the birth of Isaac, but it was the culmination of many small victories and enduring faith. Her laughter at Isaac's birth wasn't just about the miracle itself but also the countless moments of hope and trust in God's promises. Sarah's journey to motherhood was filled with years of waiting, uncertainty, and even doubt. Yet, each step of the way, she held onto the promise that God had made to her and Abraham. Her eventual joy was a testament to the faithfulness of God and the importance of holding onto hope, even when the outcome seems distant or improbable.

In my own journey, I've learned to treasure the small wins. When my baby finally slept for four hours straight, it felt like a miracle. Another time, my toddler finally said "mama" after months of babbling. These simple moments brought tears to my eyes, not just because of the words or sleep, but because they reminded me of the journey we had been on together—the sleepless nights, the endless diaper changes, the moments of frustration and joy—and how God's presence had been with us through it all.

These small wins are like God's whispers to us, reminding us that we are not alone. They can be as simple as a peaceful nap time, a hearty baby giggle, or a moment of quiet in the midst of a hectic day. Each of these moments is a precious gift, a small reminder of God's love and grace.

Mom's Moments

Take a photo of a recent small win, like your baby's smile or a moment of peace. Print it out and place it somewhere you can see daily, like the fridge or your mirror. Each time you see it, offer a quick prayer of thanks and reflect on God's presence in that moment.

Short Prayer

Dear God, help me to recognize and celebrate the small wins in my parenting journey. Thank You for Your constant presence and the joy You bring through these moments. Amen.

_____

_____

_____

50

BEING GRATEFUL FOR MOTHERHOOD

___ / ___ / _____

"And Hannah prayed and said, 'My heart exults in the Lord; my horn is exalted in the Lord. My mouth derides my enemies, because I rejoice in your salvation.'"

— 1 SAMUEL 2:1 (ESV)

Have you ever paused to consider what you are most grateful for in your journey as a mother? Is it those serene moments in the early morning when your baby is nestled in your arms, their tiny heartbeat fluttering against yours? Or perhaps it's the sound of their laughter filling your home, a joyous melody that seems to echo the love of God. Gratitude in motherhood can transform overwhelming moments into blessings.

Hannah's story in the Bible is a powerful testament to the importance of gratitude. After years of heartache and fervent prayer, God blessed her with a son, Samuel. Hannah's response was a beautiful prayer of thanks, expressing her deep gratitude and joy in the Lord. She didn't just rejoice in the gift of her son; she praised God for His faithfulness and provision. In her prayer, she acknowledged the strength and salvation that comes from God, showing us that gratitude is not just about the blessings we receive, but about recognizing the giver of those blessings.

In the whirlwind of diapers, sleepless nights, and endless feedings, it's easy to get lost in the daily grind and forget to pause and give thanks. Yet, it's in these moments that we can find true contentment and joy.

It's 3 AM, and you've just finished another feeding. You're beyond exhausted, your eyes are heavy, and your bed is calling your name. But then, you look down and see your baby's peaceful face, their tiny hand gripping your finger. In that moment, a wave of gratitude might wash over you. Despite the fatigue, there's a reminder of the precious gift in your arms. That's the essence of Hannah's prayer—finding joy and gratitude even in the most challenging times.

As a mother, I've found that gratitude can be as simple as a whispered prayer or a journal entry. Like Hannah, we can find strength and peace by focusing on God's blessings, even in the hardest times. This perspective takes intentional effort, but it allows us to see God's hand in every moment.

Gratitude in motherhood is a daily practice. It's about finding joy in the small victories, like your baby's first smile, and the significant milestones, like their first steps. It's about appreciating the support of your family and friends, and the unexpected kindness of strangers. Each of these moments is a reminder of God's love and provision.

Mom's Moments

Write a letter to someone who has been a blessing in your motherhood journey. It could be a friend, family member, or even your child. Express your gratitude and share how their support has made a difference.

Short Prayer

Dear God, thank You for the precious gift of my baby and for the countless blessings of motherhood. Help me to always have a heart full of gratitude. May I see Your hand in every moment and teach my child the beauty of a grateful heart. Amen.

51

FINDING HUMOR IN EVERYDAY PARENTING

___ / ___ / _____

> *"So Sarah laughed to herself as she thought, 'After I am worn out and my lord is old, will I now have this pleasure?'"*
>
> — GENESIS 18:12

Parenthood is a journey filled with a mix of emotions—moments of exhaustion, frustration, and even doubt about how you'll make it through another day. But then, amidst the chaos, there are those priceless moments of unexpected joy that remind you of the pure delight in being a parent. These moments often come when you least expect them, and they have a way of transforming the ordinary into something extraordinary.

Imagine when you're knee-deep in a diaper change, focused on getting everything done as quickly as possible before your baby decides they're done lying still. Just when you think you've managed to avoid any mess, your little one surprises you with an unexpected spray. For a brief second, you freeze—caught off guard by the sudden turn of events. But then, something magical happens. Instead of frustration, you feel a bubbling of laughter rising up from deep within. You start laughing uncontrollably, and before you know it, tears of joy are streaming down your face. Your baby, completely unaware of the chaos they've just caused, looks up at you with wide, innocent eyes, as if to say, *"What's so funny, Mom?"*

These are the moments that make parenthood special—the moments when the love and happiness you share with your child outweigh the challenges. This joy is a gift from God, reminding us that even on the hardest days, there's room for laughter. Like Sarah, who laughed when God promised her a child—something that seemed impossible in her old age—you too might find joy in the unexpected surprises of parenthood. These moments are not just fleeting happiness but reminders of God's blessings in the most unexpected ways.

When Sarah laughed, it wasn't just out of disbelief; it was also a reflection of the joy that comes with witnessing God's promises unfold in her life. In the same way, the laughter you share with your baby reflects the fulfillment of God's promise to bring joy into your life, even in the most unexpected ways. These moments remind you that, despite the sleepless nights and endless tasks, God is right there with you, delighting in every giggle, every smile, and yes, even in every messy surprise.

Mom's Moments

Today, take a moment to reflect on a recent funny experience you've had with your baby. How did it lift your spirits and bring joy to your heart? Write it down, and the next time you feel overwhelmed, revisit this memory to remind yourself of the laughter and love that fill your journey as a parent.

Short Prayer

Dear God, thank You for the gift of laughter and the joy that my baby brings into my life. Help me to find humor in the everyday moments of parenting and to remember that Your love is present in both the challenges and the joys. Amen.

_____

_____

_____

_____

52

ACCEPTING IMPERFECTIONS AND GROWTH

___ / ___ / _____

"I am the Lord's servant," Mary answered. *"May your word to me be fulfilled."* Then the angel left her.

— LUKE 1:38

Motherhood is a wild ride, isn't it? When you first learn you're expecting, it's natural to dream of how everything will unfold. You picture yourself as the perfect mom—always patient, always knowing just what to do. You imagine your baby as the perfect little bundle of joy, rarely fussing, always adorable, and your life as this beautiful, seamless transition into motherhood.

But then reality hits—sleepless nights, endless diaper changes, and a crying baby who can't be soothed. Suddenly, you're surrounded by laundry, unwashed dishes, and a home that's far from the tidy space you envisioned. In these moments, it's easy to feel like you're falling short of the ideal mom you hoped to be.

These are the moments when the journey of motherhood really begins to reveal itself—not as a path of perfection, but as one of growth. It's in these imperfect, messy moments that we are stretched, challenged, and ultimately, shaped into stronger, more resilient versions of ourselves. The expectations we had for ourselves start to shift, and we begin to see that it's okay not to have it all together. In fact, it's these very imperfections that help us grow, both as mothers and as individuals.

Think about Mary, the mother of Jesus. When the angel appeared to her with the news that she would bear the Son of God, Mary was likely overwhelmed. She didn't have all the answers; she didn't know what the future held. But despite the uncertainty, she responded with incredible humility and faith. "I am the Lord's servant," she said, accepting her role without hesitation. Mary's journey was far from perfect—she faced challenges, fears, and unknowns—but through it all, she trusted in God's plan for her life.

As mothers, we are often faced with our own uncertainties and challenges. We may not always know the right answers or feel confident in our decisions. But like Mary, we can choose to embrace the imperfections and trust that God is guiding us through the process. Each time we feel unsure, overwhelmed, or inadequate, we have the opportunity to lean on our faith and find peace in the knowledge that we are not alone.

It's in those moments of vulnerability—when everything seems to be going wrong—that our faith can truly shine. By surrendering our need for perfection and allowing ourselves to grow through the difficulties, we open ourselves up to the grace and strength that God offers. We learn that it's okay to make mistakes, to stumble, and to get back up again. These experiences, while challenging, are also where the deepest growth occurs.

Mom's Moments

Take a moment to reflect on a recent situation where things didn't go as planned. How did your faith help you find peace? Write down your thoughts, and remind yourself that growth often comes from imperfect moments.

Short Prayer

Dear God, help me to accept the imperfections in my journey as a mother. Give me the strength to grow and the faith to trust in Your plan. Amen.

MOM POWER: REFLECT & RENEW

DATE

S M T W T F S

REFLECTION

Finding Joy in Daily Moments

Consider a daily routine or task that you find mundane. How can you infuse this moment with joy or gratitude?

_____
_____
_____

Thankfulness in Trials

Reflect on a recent trial or difficult situation in motherhood. What lessons did you learn, and what are you thankful for despite the challenges?

_____
_____
_____

PLANNING AHEAD

Gratitude Walks

Plan a gratitude walk with your child. What sights, sounds, or experiences do you notice that remind you of God's goodness?

NOTABLE SIGHTS:

FEELINGS OF GRATITUDE:

CREATIVE ACTIVITY

Writing Letters of Gratitude

Write a letter to someone who has supported you in your motherhood journey. How has their support been a blessing, and how can you express your gratitude?

BIBLE VERSE REFLECTION

1 Samuel 2:1

And Hannah prayed and said, 'My heart exults in the Lord; my horn is exalted in the Lord. My mouth derides my enemies, because I rejoice in your salvation.'

Your Reflection

PASS ON THE BLESSINGS

"Therefore encourage one another and build each other up, just as in fact you are doing."

— 1 THESSALONIANS 5:11

Now that you've completed this devotional, you have a wealth of strength, love, and wisdom to navigate the early days of motherhood.

It's time to share your experience with others. By leaving a review, you'll help other new moms find the same comfort and guidance, passing on the blessings you've received.

Your review is a testament to your journey and a guiding light for other moms beginning their adventure into motherhood.

Thank you for your help. This journey is enriched when we share our experiences and insights with others – and you're helping to do just that.

Scan below to leave your review on Amazon:

Thank you for being a part of this community of new mothers embracing motherhood with faith and courage. May God continue to bless you and your family, and may you be a source of encouragement and light to others.

With gratitude,

Biblical Teachings

AND SO, THE JOURNEY CONTINUES...

Congratulations on embracing the profound journey of new motherhood, with all its joys and challenges. You've shown incredible strength, resilience, and grace as you've navigated sleepless nights, learned to understand your baby's signals, and balanced the demands of this new season. Whether you are savoring the quiet moments of bonding with your little one or adapting to the new rhythms of life, may your heart be filled with gratitude and hope for the future.

This journey does not conclude with the early stages of motherhood; it is the beginning of a lifelong adventure. Continue to seek God's presence in each step of your parenting journey. Let the wisdom gained from these devotions guide you as you nurture your child with love, patience, and faith. Remember the strength you discovered in yourself, the peace found in prayer, and the joy in the small, tender moments.

As you move forward, carry with you the assurance that God is with you every step of the way. Share your story, the challenges you've overcome, and the joy you've found, offering encouragement to other mothers. You are part of a community of women walking this path together, supported by God's unwavering love.

Thank you for allowing this devotional to accompany you through these early days of motherhood. It has been a privilege to walk alongside you,

AND SO, THE JOURNEY CONTINUES...

reflecting on the biblical stories of mothers like Hannah, Mary, and Jochebed, and drawing strength from their faith. May these reflections and prayers continue to provide comfort and inspiration, reminding you of God's faithful presence.

Embrace the future with confidence, knowing that God's plans for you and your baby are filled with hope and promise. The moments of feeding, soothing, and guiding your child are just the beginning of a beautiful journey. Your most rewarding days are ahead, filled with growth, love, and countless blessings.

With love and prayers,

Biblical Teachings

www.ingramcontent.com/pod-product-compliance
Lightning Source LLC
Chambersburg PA
CBHW071208070526
44584CB00019B/2964